No Earthly Estate

To me
God's truth was such a thing you could not mention
Without being ashamed of its commoness.
(*Common Beauty*)

No Earthly Estate

God and Patrick Kavanagh: *An anthology*

selected and introduced by
Tom Stack

the columba press

First published in 2002 by
the columba press
55A Spruce Avenue, Stillorgan Industrial Park,
Blackrock, Co Dublin

ISBN 1 85607 340 8

Acknowledgements

These poems of Patrick Kavanagh are reprinted with the permission of the Trustees of the Estate of the late Katherine B. Kavanagh, through the Jonathan Williams Literary Agency. The quotation from 'Religion and Literature' by T. S. Eliot is from his *Selected Prose*, and the quotation from 'Dry Salvages' is from *Collected Poems*, both published by Faber and Faber Ltd.

Texts of poems from *Ploughman and Other Poems,* Macmillan & Co Ltd, 1936; *A Soul for Sale, Poems by Patrick Kavanagh*, Macmillan & Co Ltd, 1947; *Come Dance with Kitty Stobling and other poems*, Patrick Kavanagh, Longmans, 1960; *Collected Poems, Patrick Kavanagh*, Macgibbon & Kee, 1964; *Patrick Kavanagh. The Complete Poems*, edited by Peter Kavanagh, The Goldsmith Press, 1972; *Patrick Kavanagh. Selected Poems,* edited by Antoinette Quinn, Penguin Books, 1996.

The author would like to thank the following for their help and encouragement in the preparation of this anthology: Una Agnew, Craosdella Cruess Callaghan, Antoinette Quinn and Jonathan Williams.

Designed by Bill Bolger
The cover picture is a detail from a sculpture by John Coll on the banks of the Grand Canal near Baggot Street Bridge in Dublin.
Origination by The Columba Press
Printed in Ireland by ColourBooks Ltd, Dublin

Contents

Literary criticism should be completed by criticism from a definite theological standpoint. The greatness of literature cannot be determined solely by literary standards; though we must remember that whether it is literature or not can be determined only by literary standards. I am not concerned here with religious literature but with the application of our religion to the criticism of any literature! I am convinced that we fail to realise how completely, and yet how irrationally, we separate our literary from our religious judgements. If there could be a complete separation, perhaps it might not matter: but the separation is not, and never can be, complete. The author of a work of imagination is trying to affect us wholly as human beings, whether he knows it or not; and we are affected by it, as human beings, whether we intend it or not. I suppose everything we eat has some other effect upon us than merely the pleasure of taste and mastication; it affects us during the process of assimilation and digestion; and I believe that exactly the same is true of anything we read. What I want is a literature which should be unconsciously, rather than deliberately and definitely, Christian.

— T. S. Eliot, 'Religion and Literature' in
Selected Prose

In memory of
Veronica and Kathleen

Introduction

As poets go, Patrick Kavanagh enjoys an exceptionally popular and influential place in the hearts of the Irish public. Even though Ireland can boast of two other poets who have been internationally honoured as Nobel Laureates, the Monaghan man continues to occupy a special niche in our affections.[1] Although there may be for some a quirkiness in his appeal, the fact remains that Kavanagh offers us a uniquely distilled reflection of ourselves as a people and uncovers for us an intriguing spiritual landscape, both rich and recognisable. In this his poetry is both original and enduring.

It is noteworthy that in Patrick Kavanagh's extant work of published poems, which number 253, no fewer than 138 of these include explicitly religious themes, images or allusions. This means that references to Christian faith, in one way or another, make their appearances in more than half of all his poetic writing. The religious content of his poetry is, therefore, extensive and of considerable weight. It represents a large, remarkable and even something of a self-contained segment of Kavanagh's creative work with its own particular substance and strain. It is for that reason that this collection of poems appears as an anthology in its own right.

Patrick Kavanagh himself was clear in his belief that 'poetry has to do with faith, hope and sometimes charity'.[2] Allowing that the poet's work is marked by a definite religious texture, the question may be asked whether religious faith, as it is commonly understood, can be properly embodied in poetic expression. Is this crossover possible? Can the one medium be validly apprehended in terms of the other? It has been said that 'in religion, as in poetry, we are required to make a complex act of inference and assent and we begin by taking on trust expressions which are in analogical, metaphorical or symbolic form and by acting out the claims they make: understanding religious language is a function of understanding poetic language.'[3] But poetry is not theology. The poetic statement is essentially evocative, whereas theology is discursive.

Poetry does not yield systematic statements. Rather it puts the imagination to work in an intuitive enterprise of discovery. Unlike prose, its special effect is to deliver a charge which reaches right to the marrow, so to speak, of the mind. It can stir our sensibilities often in a mysterious way, beyond the confines of rational discourse. The compound that makes real poetry does not render down to meet the requirements of raw reason. As Samuel Coleridge once remarked, 'Poetry gives more pleasure when only generally and not perfectly understood, and perfect understanding will sometimes almost extinguish pleasure.'[4] Likewise religious ideas, too, can be expressed in a manner that does not have recourse to the analytic style that we associate with strict theological investigation. Religious ideas may be conveyed in poetic form, just as poetic statement may concern itself with religious truth. Although poetic and religious discourse are distinct from one another, they are by no means mutually exclusive. In terms of meaning and appreciation, they both commonly converge.

Patrick Kavanagh's inherited and sound familiarity with his own religious tradition helps his distinctly Catholic imagination continuously to inform his poetic utterance. Nevertheless, while we engage with his personal insights on major Christian themes, we need to exercise scrupulous care to avoid colonising his 'point of view' with our own religious assumptions. This we do by preserving a fidelity to the poet's own mind and intentions and the independent provenance of his statements which are fashioned free of any institutional warrants. In deference to the poet, we shun temptations to read either too much or, for that matter, too little into his lines, never pressing his material into strict theological categories. In spite of his own stout claim that 'the poet is a theologian', this is hardly true, at least in a formal sense, although he does so often furnish us with his own formulation of the fruits of that discipline. His revelations come, as he says himself, 'as an aside'. He is never an apologist for Christian faith. His is not confessional writing. His personal dialogue with God and the sacred entices us to share it with him, precisely because it issues always from his fresh and unusual approach. He clearly communicates a definite and personal version of Christian truths but always re-formed in the poet's unique expression. It is neither false, forced nor sentimental. It is invariably simple in its depth, devoid of advocacy, always honest, sparing in style and sometimes daring in its laconic matter-of-factness. Once we accept the complexity and caprice of Kavanagh's mind, we can savour the ambiguities and elusive features of his written lines, which by turns swagger and genuflect their way into religious terrain.

It is remarkable that, in spite of the progressive distancing of Irish people from their traditional rural roots, Patrick Kavanagh's singular appeal persists among young and old alike. In an era of waning religious sensibility, his genius nevertheless continues to mine the deepest spiritual seams of our culture which, it seems, still remain precious to us, as we embark on the third millennium.

For me, Kavanagh's attraction lies, first and foremost, in the wonders of the unexpected evocations drawn from his poetic matrix of farm and field, gardens, orchards and wild flowers. I associate all these and more with charmed holidays of my youth on both banks of the river Shannon – in the County Clare of my mother's country and the West Limerick-North Kerry of my father's home. Kavanagh enlivens my recollection of pleasurable scenes, events and even my own mini-epiphanies – 'the view that happened to no one else but you' (*Our Lady's Tumbler*) – that are the stuff of the poet's patrimony. Besides, I retain the cherished memory of a rewarding, if limited, personal acquaintance with Patrick Kavanagh himself who, despite his ambiguous public reputation, I found to be a person of uncommon courtesy whose conversation I found as intriguing as it was memorable.

The Choice of Poems

The sixty poems in this selection from Patrick Kavanagh's work can be described as pointing in a religious direction, either specifically or by way of inference and atmosphere, that is, in an explicit or implicit manner. All but eight poems touch directly on Christian themes and images.[5] Those which are not overtly religious are included on the grounds that they relate to what he states is the 'spiritual quality' of his technique. An example of this may be found in the poem which bears the spiritually evocative title *Ascetic*. Although not explicitly religious, its lines offer an intimation of spiritual quest and transcendence together with its eucharistic overtone.

That in the end
I may find
Something not sold for a penny
In the slums of Mind.

That I may break
With these hands
The bread of wisdom that grows
In the other lands.

For this, for this
Do I wear
The rags of hunger and climb
The unending stair.

Another poem, *Epic*, celebrates the uniqueness and importance of all that is local. It concludes:

... I inclined
To lose my faith in Ballyrush and Gortin
Till Homer's ghost came whispering to my mind
He said: I made the *Illiad* from such
A local row. Gods make their own importance.

Kavanagh points first to the parochial setting in preference to the wider world. He insists on the particular as seedbed of the universal. Poets, in giving flesh to the word, make their own importance, as do gods ... as does the God of incarnation. For the Christian it is the mystery of God made flesh that leads to spiritual enlightenment.

Throughout the process of Kavanagh's development, we find an ironic and even playful strain which proposes a special kind of detachment and a personal indomitability in the poet. This culminates in what Kavanagh calls the 'comic vision'. But this outlook has not to do with 'funniness' as it is commonly understood, but rather with a care-free attitude, by virtue of which the poet becomes free to adopt what might be called an untroubled seriousness towards life. This worldview includes a mixture of detachment, vulnerability and hope and, as such, also informs the condition of the Christian believer. In his poem *The Self-Slaved,* we read:

No self, no self-exposure
The weakness of the proser
But undefeatable
By means of the beatable …

Steadfast fidelity to his vision ensures the poet's 'undefeatability'.

Kavanagh believed that his 'comic vision' eventually became enshrined in his literary enterprise. This he emphasised clearly and repeatedly in his prose writings.

For the reasons outlined above, each and all of the sixty poems in this collection may, I believe, contribute in one way or another to filling in the picture of religious substance which I hope may become visible through the reading of this volume. With the exception of the three long poems which, for organisational purposes, come at the end, the chosen poems are presented in the chronological order in which they originally appeared. In this way their sequence is aligned with the progressive stages of the poet's life and work.

Conventionally Patrick Kavanagh's work is divided into three periods which, in abbreviated form, run as follows: the pastoral simplicity of *The Ploughman,* the disillusionment and loss resulting from experience, and a recovered innocence and fulfilment which comes about in two distinct phases – the quest for recovery and the achievement of 're-birth'. These periods may not be regarded as watertight compartments in his poetic life. They overlap, shade into one another, sometimes erratic-ally collide and even occasionally criss-cross chronologically.

Particularity and the Christian Story

Patrick Kavanagh wrote: 'Real technique is a spiritual quality, a condition of mind or an ability to evoke a condition of mind.' One aspect of this technique was the poet's predilection for what may be called 'particularity'. The way that this technique comes into play is in his unfailing preference for the particular, which is typically expressed in a definite and concrete image, usually drawn from the most ordinary objects and events. In this way he works towards his personal, poetic insights, often reaching to a statement of arresting significance. Thus Kavanagh attempts to 'forge', as he wrote, 'a concrete, as it were, essence', by 'smelting into passion the commonplaces of life'. (*After Forty Years of Age**) The poet's concentration on particularity is a hallmark of his writing which he himself acknowledged. 'The true work of the poet is the ability to project the particular case into the larger consciousness: to show even the most insignificant detail as of universal importance.'[6] This is how Kavanagh employs his individual style in his approach to material reality, which enables him convincingly to address the transcendent dimensions of our world and our lives within it. As Seamus Heaney has said of Kavanagh: 'It is when [his] ethereal voice incarnates itself in the imagery of the actual world its message of transcendence becomes credible.'[7] The Kavanagh technique of particularity is evident in his poem *Advent*, the third stanza of which reads:

> O after Christmas we'll have no need to go searching
> For the difference that sets an old phrase burning –
> We'll hear it in the whispered argument of a churning
> Or in the streets where the village boys are lurching.
> And we'll hear it among simple decent men too
> Who barrow dung in gardens and under trees,
> Wherever life pours ordinary plenty.
> Won't we be rich, my love and I, and please
> God we shall not ask for reason's payment,
> The why of heart-breaking strangeness in dreeping hedges
> Nor analyse God's breath in common statement.
> We have thrown into the dust-bin the clay-minted wages

Of pleasure, knowledge and the conscious hour –
And Christ comes with a January flower.

The imagination's true home, to start with, is the definite image set in time. From there only can it make its way outwards and upwards from finite considerations towards the infinite and the timeless – crossing from the temporal to the eternal. This imaginative order has major implications for our understanding of the Christian way. The God of Christianity is in the first place identified through story. Out of its story emerges what we call revelation, the truths which we come to confess as the proper object of religious faith. God is characterised principally through relationships, activities and events unfolding over time, in particular situations. This story is written in the Bible, partially in the special literary genre which is termed 'spiritual language'.[8] It includes the element of mystery in its pages and it can only be fully understood and embraced when read through what we might call the lens of faith. Reflection on Christianity's origin and the manner in which it first emerged historically, confronts us with the profound drama of a definite time and place: the nativity event distinguished only by its ordinariness. It is for this reason that the birth of Jesus has been referred to as 'the scandal of particularity'. It is called 'scandalous' because it may seem that being involved in the untidiness and shame of history somehow compromises the transcendence and universality of God. This is where and how Kavanagh's poetic technique of particularity aligns itself in one sense with the story of faith.

For the Christian, the particularity *par excellence* occurs in the mystery of the incarnation through which God enters the world of the finite, becoming flesh in the person of Christ at the village of Bethlehem, some two thousand years ago.

Sacramentality

Against the backdrop of the Christian story we can begin to seek in Patrick Kavanagh's writing what it is that establishes it as an unusual repository of lively and unique features of the Catholic imagination.

There are two distinct but inter-related levels at which we find this imagination at work. First, there are those poems in which religious images and themes are explicitly and directly explored and, secondly, those in which Christian beliefs appear more obliquely.

It is at this second level that we can discover a climate of divine presence, a knack of presenting material objects as bespeaking God's handiwork and a sense of the transcendent mirrored in the physical realities of our environment. This is a poetic gift that may be described as displaying features which resemble what the Catholic tradition calls sacrament, which, in turn, gives rise to a distinct habit of religious perception known as the sacramental outlook. A sacramental perspective 'sees' the divine in the human, the infinite in the finite, the eternal in the historical. Properly understood this will never be mistaken for some kind of idolatry, pantheism or magic. True sacramentality affords the Christian believer something of a glimpse of God.

The term 'sacramentality' in the Catholic Christian tradition means the shaping of a spiritual outlook that allows created reality to exercise a symbolism enabling us to gain access to a world of spiritual realities beyond that of immediate sensory perception. In sacrament we divine God's presence in particular material entities, in events and relationships. Sacraments, in their formal and ritually designated mode, are restricted to a classical seven in number. But the notion of sacrament goes beyond the liturgical canon. In its broader sense it can be a recognition of God's presence and power implicit in and across the entire range of creation. The sacramental event or occasion does not, in any way, violate the order of material reality but endows it, by the invocation of God's word, with a new and profound layer of meaning. The sacramental vision does not tamper with or twist the integrity of God's creation. It simply enhances it. A sacrament is not some 'holy thing' arbitrarily imported from outside our universe. It is a sign elicited from creation already existing. The Christian community makes sacrament by specifying certain gifts of nature as privileged signs which, by the direct authority of Christ in the case of canonical sacraments, entitles it to read these same signs as celebration of God's love for us. Thus, our sacramental moments emerge from the already grace-filled elements of God's creation. The principle of sacramentality is rooted in the incarnation, the Word made flesh, abiding in our material world. The particular event of God taking on our flesh and blood in Jesus Christ constitutes *the* sacrament of sacraments.

Patrick Kavanagh had a special gift for investing the natural world with spiritual significance. He could turn apparently inconsequential items of every day into an experience of hope and delight. In this sense he was graced with what might be called a sacramentalising talent. Something of this illuminative skill is to be found in a number of the poems included in this selection. In the poem *A Christmas Childhood* the Epiphany event is suggested by the silhouette of 'three whin bushes' on the horizon resembling mounted figures, which represent for the poet the 'Three Wise Kings' as they approach Inniskeen, or maybe Bethlehem itself. In the poem *Kerr's Ass* naming items of a donkey's harness ingeniously moves the imagination to contemplation of 'the god of imagination'.

Parochial or Provincial

As we move away from the link which Kavanagh delicately forged between particularity and sacramentality, it is also relevant to notice the significance he attached to his mythology of the parish or local community as his own, everyone's own, enduring and special place. The parish, as the poet's irreplaceable and primary social, cultural and religious unit, is seen as a unique resource – for Kavanagh, replete with rich significance. As such, it is another symbol for him of particularity. Paradoxically it represents that which is both limited and limitless. The parochial, as he understands it, is contrasted with the provincial, which is the indeterminate and unremarkable territory, together with the unimaginative mindset that, as he believed, goes with it. He wrote: 'Parochialism and provincialism are opposites. The provincial has no mind of its own; he does not trust what his eyes see until he has heard what the metropolis, towards which his eyes are turned, has to say on any subject. This runs through all activities. The parochial mentality, on the other hand, is never in doubt about the social and artistic validity of his parish.'[9] Moreover he claims, 'Parochialism is universal; it deals with fundamentals.' This perception coincides with the task of the poet which is that of transforming apparently insignificant places and events into symbols resonant of larger truths. There is an insistence always on the potential for movement from micro- to macro-cosmic relevance in the unique resources of the local milieu. This emerges in poems such as *Epic* and both the *In Memory of My Mother* poems in each of which homely and domestic episodes lead on to statements of wider significance and enduring reality.

Three foundational doctrines of Christianity are encompassed in Patrick Kavanagh's work. These are creation, incarnation and redemption. These are not dealt with in a conventional manner but are imaginatively presented by way of his own unique poetic vision. All three infiltrate his poetry in a personal and intriguingly original manner.

Creation

Kavanagh's approach to the theme of creation corresponds closely in its inspiration to the scriptural notion of a pre-existent creative Word, or *Logos*, as it is classically termed. It is this which, in the Christian tradition, establishes the design and pattern of the universe and reveals to us the purposes of God as its creator. In the biblical account, this generative Word, together with its incarnation in time, within our world, is to be found in the Prologue of St John's gospel: 'In the beginning was the Word, the Word was with God and the Word was God. He was in the beginning with God. All things came into being through him, and without him not one thing came into being. What has come into being in him was life, and the life was the light of all people.'

In the Irish language the strongest term for 'word' is *briathar* which is the same word used for 'verb', that which entails action or that which happens. In the original Hebrew of the Book of Genesis the term used for the Word likewise denotes action, which is creative, continuous and providing. This creative Word of God is the source and instrument of God's own poetry in which we human beings are analogously invited to share. But the creative Word or *Logos*, the eternal, utterly 'other' God of the Christians does not remain detached in some cosmic solitude but breaks into our physical, sensible world at a moment of historical time in a specific place, which we have come to know as the mystery of the incarnation. 'The Word was made flesh and dwelt among us.' This, in the Christian perspective, is the definitive graced and truth-bearing event as narrated at the very beginning of the gospel of St John.

Incarnation

The incarnation of the Word ushers in a new world of hope and meaning, destined to be completed in the redemptive death and resurrection of Jesus. This is the restoration of 'all things in Christ' (cf Ephesians 1:9) fulfilled in what is called the paschal mystery.[10] These events reveal for the Christian a spiritual panorama filled with the prospect of fresh and freely conferred significance: a new gift of God unfolding for every last human being and, indeed, in its own way, embracing every single created physical entity and item in our universe. This healing and revaluation touches every tiniest crevice of creation. This we believe is so, now that the person of the all-holy God breathes intimately among and within us. God is no longer remote, unimaginable, vague and outside our ken. By virtue of his identifying totally with our flesh and blood, he has become, as we say, 'one of our own'. The implications of the incarnation are manifold and they embrace all created Being and that in the entirety of its detail. Although the mystery of God is addressed in human terms by our imagination, it must be by the genuinely grounded imagination and not the imagination of make-believe. When we speak and think of God in human categories, as we must, our biggest problem is in trying to visualise, and even somehow comprehend, the divine in terms of the insufficient power of our finite minds. God, by definition, must always remain in essence outside the reach of the human intellect. God-language can only be embarked on by way of analogy, that is, by similarity and dissimilarity held in tension by the realistic imagination.

Historically, the human quest for God has tended to take either one or other of two routes. One is by way of the exaggeratedly 'spiritualising' tendency, which operates in such soft focus and widely angled lens that it misses particularity and eschews all that is definite, resulting in a pseudo God, who is so ethereal that it is ultimately ephemeral. The authentic Christian way is rather the long plod through our material world, through our lived lives, with all the ordinariness, puzzlement and pain that this entails. In other words, the incarnational way.[11]

Perhaps it was in this context that the Anglican Archbishop Temple once offered the cheery paradox when he observed: 'One ground for the hope of Christianity lies in the fact that it is the most avowedly materialist of all the great religions.' By which he meant, I suggest, that Christian belief in creation, incarnation and redemption makes for a profound respect for nature, time and history. It is at our peril that we attempt to leap-frog over the finite and the temporal in our journey towards the Absolute. If we take God out of our world and consign him to some cloudy, celestial sphere, where he becomes altogether inaccessible, then he is effectively banished from our real lives.

Patrick Kavanagh reminds us of this when he writes in his poem *Sensualist*:

Do not stray
In the abstract temple of love.
There are no priests on the altars
Of Metaphysic
You have heard this truth before
Well, what matter!
Is the Body not the temple of the Holy Ghost
And flesh eyes have glimpsed Truth.

Redemption

Kavanagh's approach to the theme of redemption finds expression in the language of spiritual re-birth. As in the themes of creation and incarnation, redemption is interwoven symbolically with the thread of innocence – a recurring *leitmotif* of the poet's religious sensibility. This state or condition of childhood innocence makes for a quality of knowing that is conducive to an immediate recognition of primal truth and beauty, which flows from the mystery of redemption. It must be noted that Kavanagh'ss celebration of redemption is never attempted through 'Easter' poems. In one indirect, but arresting, allusion to the resurrection, he writes that after Calvary 'Men were afraid With a new fear, the fear Of love. There was a laugh freed For ever and for ever.' (*Lough Derg*) God's love for his people is established definitively by the resurrection. The assurance conveyed through the experience of the new 'freedom of the children of God' (Rom 8:21) perhaps brings with it an intimation of the comic vision so dear to Kavanagh's heart – itself offering an earnest of redemption.

However, Kavanagh does not poetically explore the mystery of the resurrection of Christ in any memorable way. This may be connected with the manner in which his religious imagination was stocked during his schooling in Christian doctrine. In his time Patrick would have acquired a brand of religious knowledge which stressed dependence on the suffering and death of Christ as the ground and source of man's salvation. The doctrine of the resurrection would have been learned primarily as a proof of the divinity of Christ rather than as the keystone of all Christian life.

On Kavanagh's redemptive horizon there is a tension between both the creational and incarnational presence of God in our world and the event of Calvary with its salvific consequences. The first-graced beauty of nature, intimately touched by the divine, through the power of the Word, had brought forth in Kavanagh's words 'a suddenness of green and light' that pre-dated the crucifixion: 'All that was true before the piteous death of the cross.' (*Why Sorrow?*)

The trajectory of Kavanagh's religious imagination leads him to chose nativity scenes in order to express ideas of redemption and spiritual regeneration. His version of spiritual regeneration, moreover, takes the form of the mystery of the re-birth of innocence. The nativity theme, which embodies the gift of new beginnings for mankind, is by its nature lyrical – the divine infant and the circumstances of his birth in Bethlehem. Foremost among these nativity poems is *A Christmas Childhood.* This taps a wellspring of seasonal sentiment and succeeds by virtue of the delicate evocation of place and expectant atmosphere. The linking of images from farming activities and local colour with the birth of Christ connects his native Inniskeen with Bethlehem, and the historical nativity event with contemporary life. In another strong poem, *Advent,* Kavanagh builds up the sense of mystery and wonder as the Christian prepares for the coming of the Saviour. God's presence among his people is renewed by the nativity. The recharging of creation with the divine presence puts 'newness ... in every stale thing'. (*Advent*)

In the sonnet *Canal Bank Walk,* with its waters 'pouring redemption', we are plunged again into baptismal sacramental imagery. The sacrament of Christian initiation by which one is re-born, as the liturgy says, 'To a new innocence by water and the Holy Spirit', and from which flows spiritual renewal, is central to the poem. Again we note that the baptismal motif is delivered in a way re-formed, as always, by the poet's imagination:

O unworn world enrapture me,

... give me ad lib

To pray unselfconsciously with overflowing speech

For this soul needs to be honoured with a new dress woven

From green and blue things and arguments that cannot be proven.

In his poem entitled *Is* Kavanagh touches on the baptismal image of water:

Mention water again

Always virginal,

Always original,

It washes out Original Sin.

While the wide sweep of Patrick Kavanagh's poetry covers the three major Christian themes which we have dealt with above, it is to be re-emphasised that they occur not in conventional or systematic theological form but rather in a free ranging fashion, inventively conceived and with constant dashes of originality which issue always from the poet's unusual 'point of view', as he himself reminds us.

Trinity

The elaborate theology of the Trinity need not concern us but its role in Christian tradition is noted since it is a recurring, important religious archetype appearing in one way or another throughout Kavanagh's poetry and he has frequent recourse to its versatility as a basic model of Christian faith and imagination. Refinements of the doctrine of the Blessed Trinity may appear so abstruse as to be off-putting and to some may seem to verge even on the fanciful. But it remains, for all that, a primordial entity that captured the poet's intuitive powers. For the believer it constitutes an image, a concept, a reality and thus a truth, by which it becomes too a source of prayerful reflection.

The term Trinity itself, growing from its biblical rudiments, dates from the 200s AD. At the Council of Nicea in 325 a clear definition of the Blessed Trinity was formally professed, as it is still to our day, in the Nicene Creed which is recited at Sunday Mass everywhere and nowadays, indeed, professed across a wide spectrum of other Christian traditions.

The salient point arising from Christian teaching on the mystery of the Trinity is that at the very heart of the Godhead we find relationship – a relationship of absolute loving. This it is that constitutes the innermost nature of the Christian God. God though one, is nevertheless also a community, a community of love. Thus God is not to be found in solitary confinement, but always and forever communally, in the company of each person, Father, Son and Holy Spirit. Moreover, the model of a triune God discloses an important practical truth which supplies the context for ordinary Christian living – that is in relationship with others. Normally, there cannot ever be what one might call 'a solitary Christian' because he or she will always be called to exercise faith, hope and love precisely as a member of a community, large or small, be it in marriage, in a family, among neighbours or, more exceptionally, within a religious congregation. Yet another dimension of the Blessed Trinity is that Christian teaching asserts that the triune God dwells through faith in the depths of each individual person. (cf John 14:23)

This profound reality for the Christian becomes the ground and guarantee of the absolute value of every human being and the ultimate source of self-esteem.

The traditional paradigm, offered by way of human representation of the triune God of Christianity, depicts the Father as Creator, the Son as Redeemer and the Holy Spirit as Sanctifier. Christian writers have always sought and gleaned a wide variety of insights to the nature of the Godhead. In their exploration of the mystery, theologians from different cultural backgrounds and in successive historical eras have constantly propounded new and differing views as to how aspects of divinity may be apprehended and explained. All these attest to the richness and vitality of the enquiring mind of faith as it scrutinises the one and same inexhaustible Reality. From earliest times two distinct currents of thought regarding the trinitarian God flow from the east and the west, the Greek and Latin traditions. Just as in our own time Kavanagh ploughed his unusual religious furrow, so on the grand cerebral scale did noteworthy scholars from different philosophical and theological traditions, east and west, attempt to disclose in meticulously analytic writing, the truth of God implicit in the Bible. From apostolic times, through the Greek and Latin fathers of the church, the medieval schoolmen, Reformation figures and outstanding modern scholars, the tradition of wisdom on the trinitarian God has evolved. In its time the Christian community has wrestled with the great heresies, as well as accommodating the sometimes idiosyncratic but precious religious input from saints and mystics.[12] Each in his or her own way, including the poet, has sought elucidation of the mystery of God whom Kavanagh acknowledges as 'the One and the Endless, the Mind that has baulked / The profoundest of mortals.' (*The One*)

References to the mystery of the Trinity are woven through Christian culture in general, and through the Irish religious tradition in particular. They appear frequently in St Patrick's *Confessio* (5th century) which is a foundational document witnessing to Irish Christianity. Historically the Trinity has given its name to numerous institutes of learning. It surfaces in popular culture as sportsmen and women 'bless themselves' in contest, while children become acquainted with the Trinity in their very first religious lessons and prayer: 'In the name of the Father and of the Son and of the Holy Spirit.'

Kavanagh invoked trinitarian images in a personal way and in this displayed a predilection for the Word and the Holy Spirit which he renders by its older title, the Holy Ghost. Whereas the Father is usually associated with creation, the Word with the Son, the second person as pre-existent to the incarnation, and the Holy Spirit with the life of holiness, yet the Spirit is also understood as the creative agent interchanging with the originating Word, made flesh in the person of Jesus Christ. The activities of each person of the Trinity may be attributed to the others. The distinction of persons does not exclude or restrict their exchange of functions. Three in One, One in Three. Patrick Kavanagh's simple, but profound, 'geometric' poem *The Circle* celebrates the Blessed Trinity into whose mystery the poet draws all of life.

God's Presence in the World

We read in Kavanagh's novel *Tarry Flynn*: 'He [Tarry, the author's *alter ego*] organised his will for a remarkable statement. "The Holy Ghost is in the field" he said in even cold tones.' This proclamation of Tarry Flynn dumbfounded his mother to whom he spoke it in the story. It was not a normal observation from your average young farmer in County Monaghan. In his poems Kavanagh again echoes Tarry Flynn's pronouncement in a slightly different key: 'Over the kind brown earth we bend and one with God we are.' (*One with God**) And again he affirms that God is 'not the abstract creator but he who caresses the daily and nightly earth.' (*Miss Universe*) Elsewhere he shares with us his conviction that 'poetry is a mystical thing'.

Arising from this testimony two issues emerge: one, the general question on the nature of our relationship to God, and the other more specific matter of mysticism as a component of that relationship. A special awareness and sense of a divine energy and presence in nature around us can create an ambience and experience which may bring the mystery of God close to us in a relationship of startling familiarity and accessibility. This sharpened cosmic consciousness in concentrated form may tempt us to simply identify God without remainder, with aspects of landscape, or with particular emanations from another human person or from privileged encounters or events of one kind or another. This represents one extreme end of the spectrum of religious experience, which has been traditionally known as pantheism. This reduces God to a form of created finite being and abolishes the idea of a God who is infinite, transcendent Being. God, understood as subsistent Being itself, on the other hand, means that God remains distinct from creatures and creation. Being, uncreated and infinite, establishes God as transcendent.

The classical Christian understanding of the deity, however, is that God is at once both transcendent *and* immanent; simultaneously 'beyond' and 'within', both separate and indwelling. This radical paradox surpasses what Kavanagh himself termed 'crude reason' and is at the heart of the God question. In effect God would not be God if the apparatus of human intellect were able fully to comprehend his mystery. Paradoxes, or apparent contradictions, are soon unearthed when we try to investigate the nature of God in order to express it in human language. All we say of him is true and at the same time untrue. He is what we say and yet he is not. Our attempt to take his measure, though often enlightening, is ultimately futile because he is by definition immeasurable. In this respect Patrick Kavanagh offers us a poetic couplet, both tart and exact: 'They had the wrong ideas of a god who once all known becomes ridiculous.' (*The Hero**) Yet we can know something, even a good deal about God without knowing him absolutely. That latter achievement remains his own exclusive prerogative. Only God knows God and only God speaks of God truly, as he does, in fact, to us through his self-revelation. He speaks to us through his creation in which he is manifest, through his word through which he is revealed and through the Spirit by which he shares with us his image.

Kavanagh's religious instinct, as expressed by his phrase 'one with God we are', (*One with God**) has prompted the view that his religious tendency was pantheistic – that he collapses the distinction between the transcendence and immanence in God. Both aspects of the supreme being must be accorded equal status and importance. God is unconditioned Being who, at once, both permeates and transcends his creation, including the human person. Because of this irreducible complementarity there is no standpoint from which we can look at God objectively in what we might call a detached manner. God is always present within us as within his creation, even before we begin the process of trying to come to terms with his reality and our knowledge and experience of him. Accordingly, everything we say about God can be translated into a declaration concerning our own existence. To talk about God then is to talk about ourselves as well. The word of God is not a message given from some outside, heavenly perch, but simply the communication of God himself who is neither on the 'out' or the 'in' side, but on both. God becomes present in us, not as some extrinsic, abstract power but is actually present at the very core of our being. His presence, therefore, pertains essentially to the very definition of human existence. A helpful distinction which banishes the pantheistic suspicion, which has been referred to in the case of Kavanagh, is the difference between a God reduced to created, finite being and a God in whom all being is included. This distinction secures the critical difference between saying 'Everything is God and God is everything' and saying 'God is in everything and everything is in God'. The preposition 'in' transforms the meaning of the latte. thus aligning it with the Pauline expression of God as 'all in all'. (1 Cor 15:28) I believe that a close reading of Kavanagh's poetry, in combination with his prose, confirms the view that his God-talk preserves a delicate, but firm, balance between God's transcendence and immanence in line with accepted Judaeo-Christian tradition.

I have rehearsed the standard Christian view of how God may be understood, not to introduce a metaphysical flourish but simply to advert to the important issue of what Kavanagh's grasp was of an elementary truth of his Christian faith. To my mind, at least, it is unlikely that he departed in any serious manner from the fundamental religious understanding he had imbibed in his parish and in his local school.[13] In company with every normal person, Patrick Kavanagh would, it is to be presumed, have entertained doubts before the paradoxes of God and Christianity. The experience of scepticism, some would argue, is actually a necessary ingredient of an authentic belief. Kavanagh's approach to religious faith was perspicacious and also intuitional as ultimately it always is for everyone. Nowhere, it would seem, does the believing intelligence desert him. It shimmers in a uniquely personal fashion throughout his public work.

He was not given to addressing his attention to the God of the philosophers or of the theologians. His imaginative faith worked rather on the God of the poets which, in turn, steered him inevitably towards the God of the mystics. Kavanagh once declared: 'Now I must search until I have found my God'. (*God in Woman*)[14] This search undoubtedly led him to the fields, to the brown earth and to silence, each of which he explicitly mentions in this context. Was he, in some way, following in the footsteps of the early Irish monks whose poetry revelled in the enchantment of nature, which touched them as an intimation of the one true God? In *The Great Hunger* he wrote:

Yet sometimes when the sun comes through a gap
These men know God the Father in a tree:
The Holy Spirit is the rising sap,
And Christ will be the green leaves that will come
At Easter from the sealed and guarded tomb.

The Poet and Prophesy

There is a school of thought which makes much of Kavanagh's mystical tendency and aptitude. Its evaluation of Kavanagh under this rubric is, after all, only to repeat what he himself averred concerning all poetry, that it is 'a mystical and dangerous thing'. But his second adjective here is perhaps as important as his first. The 'dangerous' side of poetry, which he would also claim to be mystical, may be realised in two ways: one as prophetic, and the other as misleading. Kavanagh himself speaks of the role of prophet, referring to 'the hard edged words of reality' which issue from the downtrodden, that 'arrive by the stone stairway step a day, … calling on the spirit of Prophesy to witness their despair'. Again, he invoked a moment that 'lifted a prophesy out of the clayey hours'. (*The Great Hunger*)

As to the function of the prophet we have no less than Jesus Christ's own foreboding concerning the destiny which awaits him. His proclamations are calculated to disturb not only the political, but also the cultural *status quo*. His awkward truths subvert comfortable positions and may force elites to reflect anew on established views. Jesus reproached his hearers whose fathers, he recalled, had stoned the prophets and reminded them of the perilous outcome of the prophet's utterance – the nearer he got to home, the closer his words came to the bone. Kavanagh's swiping condemnations in *The Great Hunger* of the emotional, spiritual, intellectual and sexual deprivation in his community, can be read as prophetic. This was a broadside fired against the dominant social forces of his time and place, both of his church and the received views of the wider community in which he lived. 'And the chapel pressing its low ceiling over them.'

In the gap there's a bush weighted with boulders like morality
The fools of life bleed if they climb over.

…

O to be wise
As Respectability that knows the price of all things
And marks God's truth in pounds and pence and farthings.

Lines like these, announcing in the 1940s the materialism, repression and spiritual dispossession behind a façade of piety and conformity, would not endear the poet-prophet to the powers that be. The resonance of the title itself, of *The Great Hunger*, was an eloquent judgement on aspects of the times and the fate of the people among whom he lived.

There was another side to the prophetic utterance which was capable, too, of discomfiting the poet's more sophisticated public by its simple, wry and unreconstructed moral and religious recommendations. Kavanagh censured 'vain fools who will not submit to the will of God and be themselves'; recommended that 'the rest of the world should be satisfied by loving God and praising his works …'; and further thought that 'no man need be a mediocrity if he accepts himself as God has made him. God only makes geniuses. But many men do not like God's work. Every man has a purpose in life.' These basic admonitions resemble rehashed catechism answers but, alternatively, they could conceivably serve as bald titles for seminal poems by God-centred authors on the human condition! In any event, he here taunts humanity and mischievously pokes the reproach of Christian truism at a querulous and disaffected world.

Kavanagh insisted that the poet's vocation, like that of the prophet, is to confront what is shallow and unreflective. 'And that touching or stripping of the hollow heart is what the poet willy-nilly does, and is the thing that makes him hated by the world. In every poet there is something of Christ writing the sins of the people in the dust.'

The second 'danger' of poetry, especially when the muse arrogates to itself the claim to a mystical function, is that it may lead to a form of self-deception. 'The light that could be mystic or a fraud.' (*After May*) Could he be sure his experience was the 'real thing' or simply some beguiling and ultimately flimsy projection of an extra-fertile imagination? What was the true nature and source of this 'light' of his?

The Poet and Mysticism

The God of the mystics is closest of all to the God of the poets and it is he, of course, whom Kavanagh addresses. Both the mystical and poetic way towards the knowledge of God engage us in the paradox of God's simultaneous transcendence and immanence, and our separation from, and identification with, God himself.

There is no doubt that the entire Christian enterprise for all engages us in mystery in the sense that it includes elements which go beyond what Kavanagh called 'flat common sense'.[15] The term 'mystery', as understood in the Christian tradition, is not to be regarded as off-putting. It is not a kind of grand puzzle, a zone of the absurd, nor has it anything to do with magic. It has been said that mystery is not something about which we can never know anything but rather something of which we can never know everything. Moreover, the recognition of mystery helps us to avoid placing false limits and boundaries on reality. In so far as the word mystic is related to mystery, it must be part, in some shape or form, of the experience of the ordinary reflective person.

Fundamentally mysticism may be said to be the actual experience of a loving God. Depending on the particular kind and degree of mystical experience, it can, in fact, be attributed to every and all believers across the religious divide. Alternatively it may be reserved for privileged souls whose temperament, background and training invite this as a special experience. Everyone has the experience of being somehow addressed by the mystery of God, however implicitly. The mystical experience, however inchoate, is that of a basic awareness of God. It may be disguised or hidden deep within our human activities. But the Christian, or other believer, can attend to this intimation of God and raise it to a higher and more specific level of consciousness and of explicit articulation.[16] The traditional language of the mystics, denoting an exceptional quality of prayer, is perhaps intimidating. This is classically conveyed as a contemplative movement towards God, beyond concepts and symbols – a knowledge of God by way even of unknowing.[17] Concepts and symbols lead into a darkness which is an experience of God's love in a direct and unique way. Although this remains essentially a free gift of God, one can ponder the mix of human endeavour and divine activity that furthers this experience. For Christians it should be remembered that the epitome and model of the mystic will always be Jesus Christ, whose unique intimacy with the Father was nothing less than his oneness with him. In the light of the above, one can agree that Kavanagh experienced God not only in company with his neighbours but also according to his own poetic powers and in the heightened fashion that his unusual religious imagination afforded him.

There are divergent views among theologians concerning the role of mysticism as an exceptional ingredient of the Christian life. These range from a distinct scepticism as to its value and authenticity, to an enthusiastic appreciation of its function as a credible and enduring component of the Christian way of life. Mystical experience, strictly so-called, is held in either esteem or suspicion according to the criterion which is brought to bear on the scrutiny of its characteristics. The crux of the matter seems to be that, by its very nature, the phenomenon is in itself intensely personal and exclusive to the mystic in question and so, being impossible to access from the outside, it defies objective assessment.[18]

The history of self-styled mystics and claimants to private revelations includes unhealthy aberrations of mind and heart which eventually drove men and women into an arid self-enclosure within which their spiritual energies were in the end spent unproductively, their religious eccentricity disturbing their personalities while they repeated their doomsday predictions to an uncaring world. When mysticism manifests itself in paranormal experience, it is rarely a source of genuine and enduring spiritual enlightenment. Perhaps a latter-day reluctance to acknowledge the mystical in contemporary experience is based on the proliferation of a 'token' mysticism which parades itself on occasion with bogus spiritual pretensions associated with a psychedelic culture and lacking a firm and unambiguous religious focus. But if such has earned a bad name for mysticism, it can equally be asserted that Kavanagh's poetic transcendentalism provides healthy redress, with his no-nonsense sallies into places well beyond the ordinary in a land still out of sight to the rest of us. However, it remains true that mystical flights can be risky excursions. Did even Kavanagh perhaps fear the quicksands of mysticism? After all:

God's truth was such a thing you could not mention

Without being ashamed of its commonness. (*Common Beauty**)

Yet for all its straightforward simplicity, 'God's truth' ultimately issues from the mystery of God himself. Although it might be available to one and all, nevertheless it seems to have been made manifest to Kavanagh in a unique and radical manner.

At Assisi in October 1986 Pope John Paul II met with the Dalai Lama and other world religious leaders to pray for peace. There he acknowledged publicly that people normally receive salvation through 'the sincere practice of what is good in their own religious traditions'. Later in his book *Crossing the Threshold of Hope*, he spoke of 'the common, fundamental element and the common root' of all world religions. This refreshingly inclusive statement is one important reason why a curiosity concerning mysticism leads one to first consider it in a context that goes well beyond the specifically Christian understanding of the term. Besides, I believe Kavanagh himself would have preferred to view what is called mysticism within the world religious picture. It is a strong feature of Judaism, Buddhism, Hinduism and Islam. For Hinduism and Buddhism in particular, praying to a God who is separate from ourselves does not make sense. Christian commentators would endorse this stance – as understood, however, in a conditional and clearly defined manner. We do, indeed, pray to God with whom we are one, echoing Kavanagh's poetic statement 'over the brown earth we bend and one with God we are', (*One with God**) the God of St Paul 'in whom we live and move and have our being'. (Acts 17:28) We find in the medieval Christian classic, *The Book of Privy Counselling*, the statement 'He [God] is your Being and in him you are what you are.' But another angle on the mystery comes from St John of the Cross, who spoke of God as a 'ray of darkness'. A remarkable paradox, but the world of mystical contemplation is characterised by paradoxes.[19]

The basic formulation as mentioned earlier, 'God is in everything and everything is in God', displays a unitary bias which recurs in classical mystical writing. We find it, for example, in the celebrated Meister Eckhart: 'God created all things in such a way that they are not outside himself as ignorant people falsely imagine. Rather, all creatures flow outwards but nonetheless remain in God.' Julian of Norwich declares: 'We are in God and God, whom we do not see, is in us.' The inclusive

rather than disjunctive position remains dominant in these formul-
ations of the God-creature relationship. This can be clarified if we see
God as absolute Being and although a person may be, in Kavanagh's
words, 'ablaze on the hills of Being', (*Worship*) the being of the human
creature will always be by way of finite participation in infinite Being
itself. In this way the distinction between the two does not dissolve and
there is no question of pantheism as it is commonly understood.

Underlying the ambivalence that runs through traditional mystical
expressions of the relationships between God and the human person
and vice versa is the age-old problem of the One and the many. This
ambivalence or tension can be examined in different ways, at different
levels of existence. For example, we can ask are we separate individuals
or one community in our lives and destiny? Is the believer distinct
from, or one with, God, and in what sense is he or she either one or
the other? Is every human being one with God and if so, what does
being 'one with God' mean? Is it the same as being God? The universal,
religious experience of the Absolute as the 'Other' becomes, in the
reflection of Hinduism and Buddhism, the universal One of which the
world is an illusionary manifestation.[20]

Another aspect of mysticism is the embrace of nature, that is, God's
creation as a source of rapture which, in its own way, is foremost in
Kavanagh's writing. In John of the Cross' *Spiritual Canticle* we read:

My Beloved is the mountains,

And lonely wooded valleys,

… Silent music,

Sounding solitude.

The famous Rhineland mystic and musician Hildegard of Bingen wrote:
'The Word is living, being, spirit, all verdant greening, all creativity. This
Word manifests itself in every creature.' This statement accords, in
some respects, with Patrick Kavanagh's poetic world. Moreover, it connects with the current theological concern for our natural environment.
Similarly, in our third millennium, contemplative vision, taken beyond
the cloister, impacts on social and even political issues, as indeed it

sometimes did of old. Modern mysticism, too, has made its mark in terms of peace and human solidarity issues, especially in the contemplative writings of the Trappist monk Thomas Merton. This orientation is founded on the so-called 'service mysticism' of Ignatius of Loyola, which stressed engagement with the world. This mysticism in action found its contemporary development in a special way in the cosmic consciousness of Teilhard de Chardin, for whom the world is what he named 'the divine milieu', revealing God's presence.

It is of some importance to remind ourselves again that the understanding and practice of mystical contemplation is to be found across all the great religions of the world. Interpenetrations between Buddhism, Hinduism and Christianity in the mystical realm are well documented. There is also a long and strong history of mysticism within Islam, particularly in what is called the Sufi tradition, over a thousand-year period.[21]

In yet another way, Kavanagh's poetry links with a discernible strand in classical, mystical tradition. This is his singular evocation of female images for God which is consonant with man's primordial association of life force, nutrition and healing with the female spirit.[22] For Julian of Norwich the 'motherhood of God' is enveloping, embracing, welcoming, inclusive, cosmic and expansive. Medieval Cistercian writing is also notable for female imagery occurring in its contemplative literature. Maternal images of God are closely and consistently connected with a sense of his/her presence in creation. Although, of course, it may be a truism to point out that God in his Being is beyond biological and cultural differentiation according to gender, it remains unusual and significant in twentieth-century religious usage to image God in female terms, as Kavanagh did in the poems *Miss Universe* and *God in Woman.*

Comic Vision

Arguably the most important long-term characteristics of Patrick Kavanagh's vision are, first, his progressive development as a poet and, secondly, closely related, the understanding of both his poetry and life which this development embraces. This he named the *comic vision*, the nature of which has already been mentioned. This he championed as end and fulfilment of both the poetic and the human enterprise.

> To let them see you're a living man,
> Whose comic spirit is untamed ... (*Prelude*)

Although he emphasised this comic vision in his prose writing, the implications of this personal outlook have been in the main elided by Kavanagh commentators. It is interesting, however, that in recent years, scholars have begun to pay attention to the way of comedy, in contra-distinction to that of tragedy, in both literature and theology, especially as it is specifically related to Christian belief and culture. This significant feature of Kavanagh's poetic journey may not be immediately evident to the reader and it is therefore worthwhile to attempt to make it more explicit. The comic vision of life emerges with subtlety but unusual force in the totality of his writing. Its instruments are irony and paradox. It is marked by independence and energy. Its hallmark is insouciance and its goal simplicity.

Kavanagh wrote: 'There is only one Muse, the comic muse. In tragedy there is always something of a lie. Comedy is abundance of life.'[23] Again, he singularly observed: '*The Great Hunger* is tragedy and tragedy is underdeveloped comedy, not fully born.' He further elaborates: 'A work that is inspired by the comic spirit has much to contend with for a work that is inspired by the comic spirit has a sense of values, of courage and rectitude – and these qualities are hated immemorially.'

Flowing from the comic vision is an attitude of detachment from both the poet's themes and from the orthodoxies of popular opinion. By the same token, it entails a particular quality of endurance. It also issues in the paradox of a seriously unserious approach to life. 'All true poets are gay, fantastically humorous.' Moreover, he deflates the conceit of self-importance. 'I fear that the mood I have been invoking may give the impression that what happened to me is important and that I am important. Nobody is important. We get to our destiny in the end. … We are satisfied with being ourselves, however small', in the face of 'the great perpetual'. In his ballad poem *If Ever You Go To Dublin Town*, he sings of himself paradoxically and with humorous undercurrent:

> He had the knack of making men feel
> As small as they really were
> Which meant as great as God had made them
> But as males they disliked his air.

So what are we to make of the comic vision 'in the profound sense' that Kavanagh proposes it? He was not the first poet to invoke this world-view. One preliminary clue as to its deeply Christian significance may be elicited from Dante's significant choice of title for his religious masterpiece, *The Divine Comedy* (not *The Divine Tragedy*). Originally it was simply called *The Comedy of Dante Aligheiri*.[24] The title is a template of its subject matter and the preoccupation of its author: the story of creation, incarnation, redemption, struggle and reward. It is the allegorical journey of mankind in hope. In spite of his avowed, hard-won condition of not caring, Kavanagh again paradoxically insists that 'The poet's comic spirit is real seriousness, the seriousness that will die for its ideal in the last ditch.' Comedy in its widest perspective has been described as 'the narrow escape into faith', the domain within which ultimate self-validation and meaning, *sub specie aternitatis*, reside. It challenges a view that looks on the world and life as devoid of radical significance, a view unsteadied by the incarnational principle as Christians understand it. The comic figure is not clothed in the unearthly magnificence of tragic heroism but in the awkward innocence of essential humanity. The tragic hero can take no refuge in the limitation of his human condition as he strains to take on the stronger force, the fate invading from the outside. In this sense he attempts somehow to desert himself, abandoning his trust in the buoyancy of human nature. The comic reaction, on the other hand, does not try to evade a frank acceptance of the status of its own finitude and powerlessness in the face of the assaults of Fate. It chooses acceptance; not a supine, but a creative acceptance. By very virtue of the acknowledgement of his limitation and vulnerability, the person grounded in the comic vision is he who, so to speak, rolls with the punches of adversity but manages in the end to win out by hook or by crook. He is a survivor. Although he may not be able to conquer the threat of suffering or extinction, he can transform it, so that it becomes something that is not final or absolute, but remains somehow provisional and indeed relative to a truth that stands yet beyond and which is ultimately deeper still. The comic response takes its stand on the bottom-most and stoutest rung of being itself. This comic mindset breeds a radical and strong sufficiency. It is anchored in the true nature of love and the power of survival.[25] For the person who retains what Kavanagh calls 'a main purpose' and lives by it, all things fall into sane perspective and acquire an imperishable meaning. In life's contest the comic personality may suffer defeat but not destruction. As Kavanagh concedes paradoxically in this regard, man remains 'undefeatable By means of the beatable'. *(The Self-Slaved)* In the light of this human strategy, the phenomenon of evil is not seen as hideous or terrifying. It is simply 'sad', viewed from the divine vantage-point. It retains the capacity to be transformed in the realm of comedy. The comic, of course, is not to be confused in this context with the merely funny. It is nothing less than a particular perspective on life that cleaves to hopefulness, come what may. This, in turn, as Kavanagh contends, summons laughter and humour as functions of the comic vision. Kavanagh insists, moreover, that 'laughter is the most poetic thing in life, that is, the right kind of loving laughter'. 'Free me,' he poetically exclaims, 'Put laughter within a lover's reach, O God.' *(Love and Laughter*)*

Among the legendary comic figures of literature in this sense are Shakespeare's Falstaff and Cervantes' Don Quixote.[26] We laugh both at and with the comic victim-victor because he is the image of ineradicable dignity and reflects in his person the climax of the incarnational mystery in which Jesus Christ himself, in his victimhood, emerges victorious over sin and death. The comic figure unmasks both the incongruous involvement of the finite with the infinite and also affirms it. He helps us to see that the grossly human and the grandly sublime are repugnantly and wonderfully mixed within us. Christian tradition in art and drama has classically exhibited the apparent incongruities of the events of man's salvation, played out cheek by jowl with a holy jocularity. How else do we read the place of gargoyles on the great cathedrals and the risible figures from the *dramatis personae* of the morality plays? Further back still a source of Catholic religious humour may be found deep in biblical tradition in which the notion of divine 'play' may be detected. There is a strand in the writings of the Greek fathers of Christianity which depicts creation as God at play – the creative *Logos* active, not out of necessity but out of freedom and divine spontaneity. Even the Hebrew word in the Book of Proverbs describing the activity of the Word can more precisely be translated as 'dance', the same word used in the Book of Samuel to describe David's notorious dance before the Ark of the Lord. 'All true poems laugh inwardly out of grief-born intensity,' (*Prelude*) declares Kavanagh, even as he invites us to 'come dance with Kitty Stobling', (*Come Dance with Kitty Stobling**) the name here given to his dearly beloved comic muse.[27]

In this view, the culture of the comic may be summed up in the notion that, for both Christianity and for the true poetic sensibility, nothing in life should be taken too seriously. At the same time it has to be emphasised that seriousness is never the opposite to comedy. This world is important but not ultimately so. We can step back from our religious symbols while we continue to live within them. Thus, for the Christian, the comic is rooted in faith, and laughter is the voice of faith. For this reason it can be argued that the comic spirit, comprehensively understood, is somehow closer to Christianity than is the tragic. Of the two it better offers a direction by which we may enter the gravitational field of the Spirit which, in turn, coaxes us towards our final end and destiny. In the words of Kavanagh's own rudimentary admonition, 'Only they who fly home to God have flown at all.' (*Beyond the Headlines*)

Insouciance and Simplicity

As Kavanagh finally climbs to his vantage-point on Mount Parnassus, from which he views all through the comic lens, he sees from there a 'new city' and announces that a 'free moment appears brand new and spacious, where I may live beyond the reach of desire.' (*On Reading a Book on Common Wild Flowers**) He has reached his ambition of 'not caring' and a blessed detachment. 'Why should we care? For you are at the end of all journeys by vision or prayer.' (*Drifting Leaves*)

Kavanagh confides: 'the poet's secret … is that he, in a strange way, doesn't care … He forgets himself.'[28] His condition of insouciance and self-sufficiency have helped him, most importantly, to recover long-sought simplicity. But the simplicity of his maturity is not that of his earliest period but rather that which has been distilled from the travail of his life's experience. His renewed simplicity of outlook informs his writing in what have been called his poems 'of arrival'. His early poems represented an experience of pastoral innocence; the later poems are a reflection on this experience and finally an ability to repossess it in a new mode. The moments of his personal journey have been marked by a series of situations and conditions which may be listed as follows: departure, disillusion and bewilderment, enrichment and return. Describing this spiritual odyssey, Kavanagh has himself famously explained: 'There are two kinds of simplicity, the simplicity of going away and the simplicity of returning. The last is the ultimate in sophistication. In the final simplicity we don't care whether we appear foolish or not. We talk of things that earlier would embarrass. We are satisfied with being ourselves, however small.'[29] Finally, linked with this sense of personal integration and 'at-onement' with self and perhaps too with God is the instinct that manifests itself in the motif of praise:

So be reposed and praise, praise, praise

The way it happened and the way it is. *(Question to Life)*

This couplet restfully answers his own entreaty:

… give me ad lib

To pray unselfconsciously with overflowing speech … *(Canal Bank Walk)*

In the Christian scheme the activity of praise is the highest form of prayer. It becomes possible when one has overcome excessive self-concern. Praise takes one out of oneself and into enjoyment of God and a sharing of his will for the world. Once one has entered the estate of praise an unusual form of personal change and growth may ensue. This occurs gratuitously, as by-products, so the speak, of a life simply lived. It is not something that is won by personal achievement or any work of one's own. The gift of praise unfolds the all-sufficiency of God and the gifts which he bestows. And the logic of praise is that of overflow. Praise leads to an experience of super-abundance for the one who has been 'caught' by God 'in the unconscious room Of our hearts'. *(Having Confessed)*

The Elusive Gift

Exploring the prayer of praise recalls once again the mystical 'thing' which Kavanagh claims for his poetry. In what sense can Kavanagh be described as a mystic? Who knows? It is impossible for outsiders to give a definitive answer to this question.[30] The answer, in the last analysis, can be known only to God and the poet. In attempting to explain mystical experience we are, of course, trying to describe from without that which can only adequately be described from within, which is the same as saying that only mystics themselves can ever know mysticism.

Thomas Aquinas furnishes us with a lapidary definition of mystical contemplation: it is 'the simple act of gazing on the truth', a formula that I suggest admits Kavanagh to the company of contemplatives. More restrictively, Thomas Merton tells us that 'contemplation is an awareness and realisation, even in some sense, experience, of what each Christian obscurely believes.' The special value of Aquinas' definition is that it is comprehensive enough to include the experience of both Christians and non-Christians as well as the natural contemplative experience of poets and artists. What distinguishes specifically Christian mystical experience, according to some authorities on the subject, is that it is not so much one's going out of oneself towards God, an experience of the divine, but rather God emptying himself, as it were, of his own infinity and love in order somehow to enter the here and now of our limited, human world. 'This is love, not that we love God but that he has first loved us.' (1 John 4:10) Although this activity may spring from one's own initiative, yet it will always be a gift, a sheer grace, in response to a Word first spoken by God.

This 'emptying' of God as a prerequisite of mystical prayer may perhaps question the 'natural' mysticism which is engendered by the sudden, often unexpected, ease of spirit leading to rapture, sometimes experienced through the impact of landscape, or music, or whatever else may arrest the soul. Such moments as these are evoked by T. S. Eliot in his *Four Quartets*, when he writes of

> ... the unattended
> Moment, the moment in and out of time,
> The distraction fit, lost in a shaft of sunlight,
> The wild thyme unseen, or the winter lighting
> Or the waterfall, or music heard so deeply
> That it is not heard at all, but you are the music
> While the music lasts ...

Such moments as these are classified as natural mysticism. Whether they occur by chance or as a result of conscious effort and practice, these experiences do not constitute in themselves that grace of mystical contemplation of which at least the Christian masters speak in particular. Eliot continues soberly and instructively in the same poem:

> These are only hints and guesses,
> Hints followed by guesses; and the rest
> Is prayer, observance, discipline, thought and action.
> The hint half-guessed, the gift half understood is
> Incarnation. (*Dry Salvages*)

What may happen, even to the super-sensitive soul, while sauntering through fields, may serve as a preparation for prayer or even as an accompaniment to prayer, but no degree of acquired stillness or felicity is necessarily to be construed as a form of genuine, mystical prayer. The exact status of Patrick Kavanagh's mystical moments, whether we place them in inverted commas or not, is hardly for any of us to judge. A flashing amber, if not red, light warns us against intruding on this most private and privileged area of the human soul. All we do know is that our poet did certainly pray and, moreover, that we have an inkling of what he was about when he chose to share with us his secret:

And then I came to the haggard gate
And I knew as I entered that I had come
Through fields that were part of no earthly estate. (*Tarry Flynn**)

Ploughman

I turn the lea-green down
Gaily now,
And paint the meadow brown
With my plough.

I dream with silvery gull
And brazen crow.
A thing that is beautiful
I may know.

Tranquillity walks with me
And no care.
O, the quiet ecstasy
Like a prayer.

I find a star-lovely art
In a dark sod.
Joy that is timeless! O heart
That knows God!

Ascetic

That in the end
I may find
Something not sold for a penny
In the slums of Mind.

That I may break
With these hands
The bread of wisdom that grows
In the other lands.

For this, for this
Do I wear
The rags of hunger and climb
The unending stair.

To a Child

Child do not go
Into the dark places of soul,
For there the grey wolves whine,
The lean grey wolves.

I have been down
Among the unholy ones who tear
Beauty's white robe and clothe her
In rags of prayer.

Child there is light somewhere
Under a star,
Sometime it will be for you
A window that looks
Inward to God.

I May Reap

I who have not sown,
I too
By God's grace may come to harvest
And proud,
As the bowed
Reapers
At the Assumption
Murmur thanksgiving.

A Prayer for Faith

O give me faith
That I may be
Alive when April's
Ecstasy
Dances in every
White-thorn tree.

O give me faith
That I may see
The angel of
The mountainy
Places of Dream's
Infinity.

To the Man After the Harrow

Now leave the check-reins slack,
The seed is flying far today –
The seed like stars against the black
Eternity of April clay.

This seed is potent as the seed
Of knowledge in the Hebrew Book,
So drive your horses in the creed
Of God the Father as a stook.

Forget the men on Brady's hill.
Forget what Brady's boy may say
For destiny will not fulfil
Unless you let the harrow play.

Forget the worm's opinion too
Of hooves and pointed harrow-pins,
For you are driving your horses through
The mist where Genesis begins.

Shancoduff

My black hills have never seen the sun rising,
Eternally they look north towards Armagh.
Lot's wife would not be salt if she had been
Incurious as my black hills that are happy
When dawn whitens Glassdrummond chapel.

My hills hoard the bright shillings of March
While the sun searches in every pocket.
They are my Alps and I have climbed the Matterhorn
With a sheaf of hay for three perishing calves
In the field under the Big Forth of Rocksavage.

The sleety winds fondle the rushy beards of Shancoduff
While the cattle-drovers sheltering in the Featherna Bush
Look up and say: 'Who owns them hungry hills
That the water-hen and snipe must have forsaken?
A poet? Then by heavens he must be poor.'
I hear and is my heart not badly shaken?

Worship

To your high altar I once came
Proudly, even brazenly, and I said: –
Open your tabernacles I too am flame
Ablaze on the hills of Being. Let the dead
Chant the low prayer beneath a candled shrine,
O cut for me life's bread, for me pour wine!

Inniskeen Road: July Evening

The bicycles go by in twos and threes –
There's a dance in Billy Brennan's barn tonight,
And there's the half-talk code of mysteries
And the wink-and-elbow language of delight.
Half-past eight and there is not a spot
Upon a mile of road, no shadow thrown
That might turn out a man or woman, not
A foolfall tapping secrecies of stone.

I have what every poet hates in spite
Of all the solemn talk of contemplation.
Oh, Alexander Selkirk knew the plight
Of being king and government and nation.
A road, a mile of kingdom, I am king
Of banks and stones and every blooming thing.

April

Now is the hour we rake out the ashes
Of the spirit-fires winter-kindled.
This old temple must fall,
We dare not leave it
Dark, unlovely, deserted.
Level! O level it down!
Here we are building a bright new town.

That old cranky spinster is dead
Who fed us cold flesh.
And in the green meadows
The maiden of Spring is with child
By the Holy Ghost.

March

The trees were in suspense,
Listening with an intense
Anxiety for the Word
That in the Beginning stirred
The dark-branched Tree
Of Humanity.

Subjectively the dogs
Hunted the muted bogs,
The horses suppressed their neighing,
No donkey-kind was braying,
The hare and rabbit under –
Stood the cause of wonder.

The blackbird of the yew
Alone broke the two
Minutes' silence
With a new poem's violence.
A tomboy scare that drove
Faint thoughts to active love.

After May

May came, and every shabby phoenix flapped
A coloured rag in lieu of shining wings;
In school bad manners spat and went unslapped –
Schoolmistress Fancy dreamt of other things.
The lilac blossomed for a day or two
Gaily, and then grew weary of her fame.
Plough-horses out on grass could now pursue
The pleasures of the very mute and tame.

A light that might be mystic or a fraud
Played on far hills beyond all common sight,
And some men said that it was Adam's God
As Adam saw before the Apple-bite.
Sweet May is gone, and now must poets croon
The praises of a rather stupid June.

Sanctity

To be a poet and not know the trade,
To be a lover and repel all women;
Twin ironies by which great saints are made,
The agonizing pincer-jaws of Heaven.

Street Corner Christ

I saw Christ today
At a street corner stand,
In the rags of a beggar he stood
He held ballads in his hand.

He was crying out: 'Two for a penny
Will anyone buy
The finest ballads ever made
From the stuff of joy?'

But the blind and deaf went past
Knowing only there
An uncouth ballad-seller
With tail-matted hair.

And I whom men call fool
His ballads bought
Found Him whom the pieties
Have vainly sought.

Drifting Leaves

We drift and we care not whither,
Why should we care?
For You are at the end of all journeys
By vision or prayer.

Blow us O Wind, O blow us
Whither you will.
Every leaf that November casts clay-ward
Shall its own place fill.

To Knowledge

You taught me far too many things,
Filling my singing void
With signs and sounds until the kings
Creative could not bide.

Before you came I knew the speech
Of mountains, I could pray
With stone and water. O foul leech
That sucks truth's blood away!

The dark mysterious blind of Earth
You drew, and I could see
Only the walls of life, the girth
Of one ill-fruited tree.

You taught me how to steer by night
Unstarred and port no lie –
But my first dream had wings of light
And cherub witchery.

You said: This is the only way
Of truth. And the fool in me
Buried God's lantern in dark clay
That an angel might not see.

Truth

The light behind a written word,
The silence of a singing bird,

The quiet at the root of trouble,
Not love, but love's ecstatic double,

A child asleep upon its prayer,
The glance of eyes that do not stare,

The beauty-spell of things uncouth –
These are the marks of living truth.

The Lady of the Poets

O Lady of the lonely and unloved
You are unmoved
By the lean anguish of a poet's cry –
You have heard so many greater than I.

You I have long known
In tree and stone
And in all sealed tongues
Of sympathy. How many songs
Of secret self have you heard –
Pitiful prayers that dared
Not turn to High
Heaven for mercy?

You have listened to the great,
And yet you wait
To comfort me
In my lone house of poetry.

Ethical

You who have not sown
Will eat the bitter bread
And beg the sweetness of a stone
Flung at Saint Stephen's head.

You who have not sung
Will hear the clang of brass
When fairies beat on April's gong
With stems of greening grass.

And you who have not prayed
The blackbird's evening prayer
Will kneel all night dismayed
Upon a frozen stair.

The Circle

The Circle is the Father
Diameter His Son
Spirit the mathematical centre
Thus truth is known
In all turning wheels
In all tumbling clowns
As in the firmament deep
Where the Prophet drowns.

Blessed are the followers
Of all wheel tracks,
Blessed the spoke-tortured
Christ. The axe
Traces a circle
And in that trace
Is the power the Word
And the tortured Face.

Sensualist

Realise the touch kingdom
Do not stray
In the abstract temple of love.
There are no priests on the altars
Of Metaphysic
You have heard this truth before
Well, what matter!
Is the body not the temple of the Holy Ghost
And flesh eyes have glimpsed Truth.

Primrose

Upon a bank I sat, a child made seer
Of one small primrose flowering in my mind.
Better than wealth it is, said I, to find
One small page of Truth's manuscript made clear.
I looked at Christ transfigured without fear –
The light was very beautiful and kind,
And where the Holy Ghost in flame had signed
I read it through the lenses of a tear.
And then my sight grew dim, I could not see
The primrose that had lighted me to Heaven,
And there was but the shadow of a tree
Ghostly among the stars. The years that pass
Like tired soldiers nevermore have given
Moments to see wonders in the grass.

Christmas, 1939

O Divine Baby in the cradle
All that is poet in me
Is the dream I dreamed of Your Childhood
And the dream You dreamed of me.

O Divine Baby in the cradle
All that is truth in me
Is my mind tuned to the cadence
Of a child's philosophy.

O Divine Baby in the cradle
All that is pride in me
Is my mind bowed in homage
Upon Your Mother's knee.

O Divine Baby in the cradle
All that is joy in me
Is that I have saved from the ruin
Of my soul Your Infancy.

Christmas Eve Remembered

I see them going to the chapel
To confess their sins. Christmas Eve
In a parish in Monaghan.
Poor parish! and yet memory does weave
For me about those folk
A romantic cloak.

No snow, but in their minds
The fields and roads are white;
They may be talking of the turkey markets
Or foreign politics, but tonight
Their plain, hard country words
Are Christ's singing birds.

Bicycles scoot by, old women
Cling to the grass-margin:
Their thoughts are earthy but their minds move
In dreams of the Blessed Virgin
For one in Bethlehem
Has kept their dreams safe for them.

'Did you hear from Tom this Christmas?'
'These are the dark days.'
'Maguire's shop did a great trade,
Turnover double – so Maguire says.'
'I can't delay now, Jem
Lest I be late in Bethlehem.'

Like this my memory saw,
Like this my childhood heard
These pilgrims of the North ...
And memory, you have me spared
A light to follow them
Who go to Bethlehem.

Spraying the Potatoes

The barrels of blue potato-spray
Stood on a headland of July
Beside an orchard wall where roses
Were young girls hanging from the sky.

The flocks of green potato-stalks
Were blossom spread for sudden flight,
The Kerr's Pinks in a frivelled blue,
The Arran Banners wearing white.

And over that potato-field
A lazy veil of woven sun.
Dandelions growing on headlands, showing
Their unloved hearts to everyone.

And I was there with the knapsack sprayer
On the barrel's edge poised. A wasp was floating
Dead on a sunken briar leaf
Over a copper-poisoned ocean.

The axle-roll of a rut-locked cart
Broke the burnt stick of noon in two.
An old man came through a corn-field
Remembering his youth and some Ruth he knew.

He turned my way. 'God further the work.'
He echoed an ancient farming prayer.
I thanked him. He eyed the potato-drills.
He said: 'You are bound to have good ones there.'

We talked and our talk was a theme of kings,
A theme for strings. He hunkered down
In the shade of the orchard wall. O roses
The old man dies in the young girl's frown.

And poet lost to potato-fields,
Remembering the lime and copper smell
Of the spraying barrels he is not lost
Or till blossomed stalks cannot weave a spell.

Christmas Carol 1941

I see the North Star
And the North Star sees me,
But who sees the Star of Peace
In the East, cloudy?

I see the donkey plod
Through the deep snow,
But where can the Mother of God
In this storm go?

I see the Three Wise Kings,
They've lost their way,
Wandering around in rings
Day after day.

I see the Son of God
In the straw where he lies,
But I hear no angel sing
Peace in the skies.

I see the countless stars
And the countless stars see me,
But no one sees the Star of Peace
In the East, cloudy.

Advent

We have tested and tasted too much, lover –
Through a chink too wide there comes in no wonder.
But here in this Advent-darkened room
Where the dry black bread and the sugarless tea
Of penance will charm back the luxury
Of a child's soul, we'll return to Doom
The knowledge we stole but could not use.

And the newness that was in every stale thing
When we looked at it as children: the spirit-shocking
Wonder in a black slanting Ulster hill
Or the prophetic astonishment in the tedious talking
Of an old fool will awake for us and bring
You and me to the yard gate to watch the whins
And the bog-holes, cart-tracks, old stables where Time begins.

O after Christmas we'll have no need to go searching
For the difference that sets an old phrase burning –
We'll hear it in the whispered argument of a churning
Or in the streets where the village boys are lurching.
And we'll hear it among simple decent men too
Who barrow dung in gardens under trees,
Wherever life pours ordinary plenty.
Won't we be rich, my love and I, and please
God we shall not ask for reason's payment,
The why of heart-breaking strangeness in dreeping hedges
Nor analyse God's breath in common statement.
We have thrown into the dust-bin the clay-minted wages
Of pleasure, knowledge and the conscious hour –
And Christ comes with a January flower.

A Lover's Lenten Dream

This time when the birds are singing
Maybe I'll be sad no more
One I've waited aeons for
May be waiting at my door.

When the Lenten roots are swinging
Lamps of light above the grass
What I've dreamt may come to pass
At a holy Easter Mass.

O the growing corn and hedges
That made me want to cry
For something lost when I
Was wandering in the sky.

My birds are all in cages
Maybe now the doors will rise
And the grief that looked so wise
Dissolve in laughing skies.

Beyond the Headlines

Then I saw the wild geese flying
In fair formation to their bases in Inchicore
And I knew that these wings would outwear the wings war
And a man's simple thoughts outlive the day's loud lying.
Don't fear, don't fear, I said to my soul.
The Bedlam of Time is an empty bucket rattled,
'Tis you who will say in the end who best battled.
Only they who fly home to God have flown at all.

Christmas Carol 1942

Sing of the Childhood
That renews in our eyes
Beauty grown tired.
Tonight is inspired,
Land, sea and skies
With a Childhood surprise.

Sing of the Childhood
That renews in the heart
Of the hopeless hope's cheer;
Year after year
Giving a fresh start
Where Sin's gaolers depart.

Sing of the Childhood
That renews for us all –
Banker or farmer
Or soldier in armour –
The laugh of the soul.
Sing the Child in the Stall.

A Christmas Childhood

I

One side of the potato-pits was white with frost –
How wonderful that was, how wonderful!
And when we put our ears to the paling-post
The music that came out was magical.

The light between the ricks of hay and straw
Was a hole in Heaven's gable. An apple tree
With its December-glinting fruit we saw –
O you, Eve, were the world that tempted me

To eat the knowledge that grew in clay
And death the germ within it! Now and then
I can remember something of the gay
Garden that was childhood's. Again

The tracks of cattle to a drinking-place,
A green stone lying sideways in a ditch
Or any common sight the transfigured face
Of a beauty that the world did not touch.

II

My father played the melodion
Outside at our gate;
There were stars in the morning east
And they danced to his music.

Across the wild bogs his melodion called
To Lennons and Callans.
As I pulled on my trousers in a hurry
I knew some strange thing had happened.
Outside in the cow-house my mother

Made the music of milking;
The light of her stable-lamp was a star
And the frost of Bethlehem made it twinkle.

A water-hen screeched in the bog,
Mass-going feet
Crunched the wafer-ice on the pot-holes,
Somebody wistfully twisted the bellows wheel.

My child poet picked out the letters
On the grey stone,
In silver the wonder of a Christmas townland,
The winking glitter of a frosty dawn.

Cassiopeia was over
Cassidy's hanging hill,
I looked and three whin bushes rode across
The horizon – the Three Wise Kings.

An old man passing said:
'Can't he make it talk' –
The melodion. I hid in the doorway
And tightened the belt of my box-pleated coat.

I nicked six nicks on the door-post
With my penknife's big blade –
There was a little one for cutting tobacco.
And I was six Christmases of age.

My father played the melodion,
My mother milked the cows,
And I had a prayer like a white rose pinned
On the Virgin Mary's blouse.

Bluebells for Love

There will be bluebells growing under the big trees
And you will be there and I will be there in May;
For some other reason we both will have to delay
The evening in Dunshaughlin – to please
Some imagined relation,
So both of us came to walk through that plantation.

We will be interested in the grass,
In an old bucket-hoop, in the ivy that weaves
Green incongruity among dead leaves,
We will put on surprise at carts that pass –
Only sometimes looking sideways at the bluebells in the plantation
And never frighten them with too wild an exclamation.

We will be wise, we will not let them guess
That we are watching them or they will pose
A mere façade like boys
Caught out in virtue's naturalness.
We will not impose on the bluebells in that plantation
Too much of our desire's adulation.

We will have other loves – or so they'll think;
The primroses or the ferns or the briars,
Or even the rusty paling wires,
Or the violets on the sunless sorrel bank.
Only as an aside the bluebells in the plantation
Will mean a thing to our dark contemplation.

We'll know love little by little, glance by glance.
Ah, the clay under these roots is so brown!
We'll steal from Heaven while God is in the town –
I caught an angel smiling in a chance
Look through the tree-trunks of the plantation
As you and I walked slowly to the station.

In Memory of my Mother

Died November 10th, 1945

You will have the road gate open, the front door ajar
The kettle boiling and a table set
By the window looking out at the sycamores –
And your loving heart lying in wait

For me coming up among the poplar trees.
You'll know my breathing and my walk
And it will be a summer evening on those roads
Lonely with leaves of thought.

We will be choked with the grief of things growing,
The silence of dark-green air
Life too rich – the nettles, docks and thistles
All answering the prodigal's prayer.

You will know I am coming though I send no word
For you were lover who could tell
A man's thoughts – my thoughts – though I hid them –
Through you I knew Woman and did not fear her spell.

In Memory of My Mother

I do not think of you lying in the wet clay
Of a Monaghan graveyard; I see
You walking down a lane among the poplars
On your way to the station, or happily

Going to second Mass on a summer Sunday –
You meet me and you say:
'Don't forget to see about the cattle –'
Among your earthiest words the angels stray.

And I think of you walking along a headland
Of green oats in June,
So full of repose, so rich with life –
And I see us meeting at the end of a town

On a fair day by accident, after
The bargains are all made and we can walk
Together through the shops and stalls and markets
Free in the oriental streets of thought.

O you are not lying in the wet clay,
For it is a harvest evening now and we
Are piling up the ricks against the moonlight
And you smile up at us – eternally.

From Failure Up

Can a man grow from the dead clod of failure
Some consoling flower
Something humble as a dandelion or a daisy,
Something to wear as a buttonhole in Heaven?
Under the flat, flat grief of defeat maybe
Hope is a seed.
Maybe this's what he was born for, this hour
Of hopelessness.
Maybe it is here he must search
In this hell of unfaith
Where no one has a purpose
Where the web of Meaning is broken threads
And one man looks at another in fear.
O God can a man find You when he lies with his face downwards
And his nose in the rubble that was his achievement?
Is the music playing behind the door of despair?
O God give us purpose.

The Gift

One day I asked God to give
Me perfection so I'd live
Smooth and courteous, calmly wise
All the world's virtuous prize.

So I should not always be
Getting into jeopardy,
Being savage, wild and proud
Fighting, arguing with the crowd;

Being poor, sick depressed,
Everywhere an awful pest;
Being too right, being too wrong.
Being too weak, being too strong,

Being every hour fated
To say the things that make me hated;
Being a failure in the end –
God, perfection on me spend.

And God spoke out of Heaven
The only gift in My giving
Is yours – Life. Seek in hell
Death, perfect, wise, comfortable.

A View of God and the Devil

I met God the Father in the street
And the adjectives by which I would describe him are these:
Amusing
Experimental
Irresponsible –
About frivolous things.
He was not a man who would be appointed to a Board
Nor impress a bishop
Or gathering of art lovers.

He was not splendid, fearsome or terrible
And yet not insignificant.
This was my God who made the grass
And the sun,
And stones in streams in April;
This was the God I met in Dublin
As I wandered the unconscious streets.

This was the God that brooded over the harrowed field –
Rooneys – beside the main Carrick road
The day my first verses were printed –
I knew him and was never afraid
Of death or damnation;
And I knew that the fear of God was the beginning of folly.

The Devil

I met the Devil too,
And the adjectives by which I would describe him are these:
Solemn,
Boring,
Conservative.
He was a man the world would appoint to a Board,
He would be on the list of invitees for a bishop's garden party,
He would look like an artist.
He was the fellow who wrote in newspapers about music,
Got into a rage when someone laughed;
He was serious about unserious things;
You had to be careful about his inferiority complex
For he was conscious of being uncreative.

God in Woman

Now I must search till I have found my God –
Not in an orphanage. He hides
In no humanitarian disguise,
A derelict upon a barren bog;
But in some fantastically ordinary incog:
Behind a well-bred convent girl's eyes,
Or wrapped in middle-class felicities
Among the women in a coffee shop.
Surely my God is feminine, for Heaven
Is the generous impulse, is contented
With feeding praise to the good. And all
Of these that I have known have come from women.
While men the poet's tragic light resented,
The spirit that is Woman caressed his soul.

Epic

I have lived in important places, times
When great events were decided: who owned
That half a rood of rock, a no-man's land
Surrounded by our pitchfork-armed claims.
I heard the Duffys shouting 'Damn your soul'
And old McCabe stripped to the waist, seen
Step the plot defying blue cast-steel –
'Here is the march along these iron stones'
That was the year of the Munich bother. Which
Was more important? I inclined
To lose my faith in Ballyrush and Gortin
Till Homer's ghost came whispering to my mind
He said: I made the *Iliad* from such
A local row. Gods make their own importance.

Innocence

They laughed at one I loved –
The triangular hill that hung
Under the Big Forth. They said
That I was bounded by the whitethorn hedges
Of the little farm and did not know the world.
But I knew that love's doorway to life
Is the same doorway everywhere.

Ashamed of what I loved
I flung her from me and called her a ditch
Although she was smiling at me with violets.

But now I am back in her briary arms
The dew of an Indian Summer morning lies
On bleached potato-stalks –
What age am I?

I do not know what age I am,
I am no mortal age;
I know nothing of women,
Nothing of cities,
I cannot die
Unless I walk outside these whitethorn hedges.

Auditors In

I

The problem that confronts me here
Is to be eloquent yet sincere;
Let myself rip and not go phoney
In an inflated testimony.
Is verse an entertainment only?
Or is it a profound and holy
Faith that cries the inner history
Of the failure of man's mission?
Should it be my job to mention
Precisely how I chanced to fail
Through a cursed ideal?
Write down here: he knew what he wanted –
Evilest knowledge ever haunted
Man when he can picture clear
Just what he is searching for.

A car, a big suburban house,
Half secret that he might not lose
The wild attraction of the poor
But proud, the fanatic lure
For women of the poet's way
And diabolic underlay;
The gun of pride can bring them down
At twenty paces in the town –
For what? the tragedy is this:
Pride's gunman hesitates to kiss.

A romantic Rasputin
Praying at the heart of sin.
He cannot differentiate

Say if he does not want to take
From moral motives or because
Nature has ideal in her laws.

But to get down to the factual –
You are not homosexual.
And yet you live without a wife,
A most disorganised sort of life.
You've not even bred illegitimates –
A lonely lecher whom the fates
By a financial trick castrates.

You're capable of an intense
Love that is experience.
Remember how your heart was moved
And youth's eternity was proved
When you saw a young girl going to Mass
On a weekday morning as
You yourself used to go
Down to church from Ednamo.
Your imagination still enthuses
Over the dandelions at Willie Hughes'
And these are equally valid
For urban epic, peasant ballad.
Not mere memory but the Real
Poised in the poet's commonweal.
And you must take yourself in hand
And dig and ditch your authentic land.

Wake up, wake up and compromise
On the non-essential sides
Love's round you in a rapturous bevy
But you are bankrupt by the levy
Imposed upon the ideal:

Her Cheshire-cat smile surmounts the wall.
She smiles 'Wolf, wolf, come be my lover'
Unreal you find and yet you never
Catch on. One cannot but feel sorry,
For the ideal is purgatory.
Yet do not be too much dismayed
It's on your hand the humble trade
Of versing that can easily
Restore your equanimity
And lay the looney ghosts that goad
The savages of Pembroke Road …
Bow down here and thank your God.

II

After the prayer I am ready to enter my heart
Indifferent to the props of a reputation:
Some feeble sallies of a peasant plantation,
The rotten shafts of a remembered cart
Holding up the conscious crust of art.
No quiet corner here for contemplation,
No roots of faith to give my angry passion
Validity. I at the bottom will start
Try to ignore the shame-reflecting eyes
Of worshippers who made their god too tall
To share their food or do the non-stupendous,
They gave him for exploring empty skies
Instead of a little room where he might write for
Men too real to live by vapid legends.

Away, away on wings like Joyce's
Mother Earth is putting my brand new clothes in order
Praying, she says, that I no more ignore her
Yellow buttons she found in fields at bargain prices.

Kelly's Big Bush for a button-hole. Surprises
In every pocket – the stream at Connolly's corner,
Myself at Annavackey on the Armagh border,
Or calm and collected in a calving crisis.
Not sad at all as I float away, away
With Mother keeping me to the vernacular.
I have a home to return to now. O blessing
For the return in Departure. Somewhere to stay
Doesn't matter. What is distressing
Is waking eagerly to go nowhere in particular.

From the sour soil of a town where all roots canker
I turn away to where the Self reposes
The placeless Heaven that's under all our noses
Where we're shut off from all the barren anger,
No time for self-pitying melodrama,
A million Instincts know no other uses
Than all day long to feed and charm the Muses
Till they become pure positive. O hunger
Where all have mouths of desire and none
Is willing to be eaten! I am so glad
To come so accidentally upon
My Self at the end of a tortuous road
And have learned with surprise that God
Unworshipped withers to the Futile One.

If Ever You Go To Dublin Town

If ever you go to Dublin town
In a hundred years or so
Inquire for me in Baggot Street
And what I was like to know.
O he was a queer one,
Fol dol the di do,
He was a queer one
I tell you.

My great-grandmother knew him well,
He asked her to come and call
On him in his flat and she giggled at the thought
Of a young girl's lovely fall.
O he was dangerous
Fol dol the di do,
He was dangerous
I tell you.

On Pembroke Road look out for my ghost
Dishevelled with shoes untied,
Playing through the railings with little children
Whose children have long since died.
O he was a nice man
Fol dol the di do,
He was a nice man
I tell you.

Go into a pub and listen well
If my voice still echoes there,
Ask the men what their grandsires thought
And tell them to answer fair.
O he was eccentric
Fol dol the di do,
He was eccentric
I tell you.

He had the knack of making men feel
As small as they really were
Which meant as great as God had made them
But as males they disliked his air.
O he was a proud one
Fol dol the di do,
He was a proud one
I tell you.

If ever you go to Dublin town
In a hundred years or so
Sniff for my personality,
Is it vanity's vapour now?
O he was a vain one
Fol dol the di do,
He was a vain one
I tell you.

I saw his name with a hundred others
In a book in the library
It said he had never fully achieved
His potentiality.
O he was slothful
Fol dol the di do,
He was slothful
I tell you.

He knew that posterity has no use
For anything but the soul,
The lines that speak the passionate heart,
The spirit that lives alone.
O he was a lone one,
Fol dol the di do,
Yet he lived happily
I tell you.

Kerr's Ass

We borrowed the loan of Kerr's big ass
To go to Dundalk with butter,
Brought him home the evening before the market
An exile that night in Mucker.

We heeled up the cart before the door,
We took the harness inside –
The straw-stuffed straddle, the broken breeching
With bits of bull-wire tied;

The winkers that had no choke-band,
The collar and the reins …
In Ealing Broadway, London Town
I name their several names

Until a world comes to life –
Morning, the silent bog,
And the god of imagination waking
In a Mucker fog.

Having Confessed

Having confessed he feels
That he should go down on his knees and pray
For forgiveness for his pride, for having
Dared to view his soul from the outside.
Lie at the heart of the emotion, time
Has its own work to do. We must not anticipate
Or awaken for a moment. God cannot catch us
Unless we stay in the unconscious room
Of our hearts. We must be nothing,
Nothing that God may make us something.
We must not touch the immortal material
We must not daydream tomorrow's judgement –
God must be allowed to surprise us.
We have sinned, sinned like Lucifer
By this anticipation. Let us lie down again
Deep in anonymous humility and God
May find us worthy material for His hand.

The Son of God

He said, 'Art thou the Son of God?' expecting
'Thou has said it' – or some such words
From a humble man ashamed to admit
That he too would shoot down Pleasure's singing birds.
But I took my heart in my hands and showed it
Constricted by selfish muscles and I denied
That I was prepared to die for the sins of men;
And he tore the dust of death that was his hair and said I lied.

'He's great, he's God!' he ran through the streets telling
Everybody that would listen. I was enticed
To accept. But I dashed over the hills when they hammered the cross –
The Christ that won't die is a mean Christ.

Out beyond Calvary I found myself a house
And lived there in comfort. But I could hear
Often on summer evenings from the deserts of the heart
Of man the cry for the blood of God's only Son.

Prelude

Give us another poem, he said
Or they will think your muse is dead;
Another middle-age departure
Of Apollo from the trade of archer.
Bring out a book as soon as you can
To let them see you're a living man,
Whose comic spirit is untamed
Though sadness for a little claimed
The precedence; and tentative
You pulled your punch and wondered if
Old cunning Silence might not be
A better bet than poetry.

You have not got the countenance
To hold the angle of pretence,
That angry bitter look for one
Who knows that art's a kind of fun;
That all true poems laugh inwardly
Out of grief-born intensity.
Dullness alone can get you beat
And so can humour's counterfeit.
You have not got a chance with fraud
And might as well be true to God.

Then link your laughter out of doors
In sunlight past the sick-faced whores
Who chant the praise of love that isn't
And bring their bastards to be Christened
At phoney founts by bogus priests
With rites mugged up by journalists.
Walk past professors looking serious

Fondling an unpublished thesis –
'A child! my child! my darling son'
Some Poets of Nineteen Hundred and One
Note well the face profoundly grave,
An empty mind can house a knave.
Be careful to show no defiance,
They've made pretence into a science:
Card-sharpers of the art committees
Working all the provincial cities,
They cry 'Eccentric' if they hear
A voice that seems at all sincere.
Fold up their table and their gear
And with the money disappear.

But satire is unfruitful prayer,
Only wild shoots of pity there,
And you must go inland and be
Lost in compassion's ecstasy,
Where suffering soars in summer air –
The millstone has become a star.

Count then your blessings, hold in mind
All that has loved you or been kind:
Those women on their mercy missions,
Rescue work with kiss or kitchens,
Perceiving through the comic veil
The poet's spirit in travail.

Gather the bits of road that were
Not gravel to the traveller
But eternal lanes of joy
On which no man who walks can die.
Bring in the particular trees

That caught you in their mysteries.
And love again the weeds that grew
Somewhere specially for you.
Collect the river and the stream
That flashed upon a pensive theme,
And a positive world make,
A world man's world cannot shake.
And do not lose love's resolution
Though face to face with destitution.

If Platitude should claim a place
Do not denounce his humble face;
His sentiments are well-intentioned
He has a part in the larger legend.

So now my gentle tiger burning
In the forest of no-yearning
Walk on serenely, do not mind
That Promised Land you thought to find
Where the worldly-wise and rich take over
The mundane problems of the lover.
Ignore Power's schismatic sect
Lovers alone lovers protect.

The Hospital

A year ago I fell in love with the functional ward
Of a chest hospital: square cubicles in a row
Plain concrete, wash basins – an art lover's woe,
Not counting how the fellow in the next bed snored.
But nothing whatever is by love debarred,
The common and banal her heat can know.
The corridor led to a stairway and below
Was the inexhaustible adventure of a gravelled yard.

This is what love does to things: the Rialto Bridge,
The main gate that was bent by a heavy lorry,
The seat at the back of a shed that was a suntrap.
Naming these things is the love-act and its pledge;
For we must record love's mystery without claptrap,
Snatch out of time the passionate transitory.

Is

The important thing is not
To imagine one ought
Have something to say,
A raison d'être, a plot for the play.
The only true teaching
Subsists in watching
Things moving or just colour
Without comment from the scholar.
To look on is enough
In the business of love.
Casually remark
On a deer running in a park;
Mention water again
Always virginal,
Always original,
It washes out Original Sin.
Name for the future
The everydays of nature
And without being analytic
Create a great epic.
Girls in red blouses,
Steps up to houses,
Sunlight round gables,
Gossip's young fables,
The life of a street.

O wealthy me! O happy state!
With an inexhaustible theme
I'll die in harness,
I'll die in harness with my scheme.

To Hell with Commonsense

More kicks than pence
We get from commonsense
Above its door is writ
All hope abandon. It
Is a bank will refuse a post
Dated cheque of the Holy Ghost.
Therefore I say to hell
With all reasonable
Poems in particular
We want no secular
Wisdom plodded together
By concerned fools. Gather
No moss you rolling stones
Nothing thought out atones
For no flight
In the light.
Let them wear out nerve and bone
Those who would have it that way
But in the end nothing that they
Have achieved will be in the shake up
In the final Wake Up
And I have a feeling
That through the hole in reason's ceiling
We can fly to knowledge
Without ever going to college.

Miss Universe

I learned, I learned – when one might be inclined
To think, too late, you cannot recover your losses –
I learned something of the nature of God's mind,
Not the abstract Creator but He who caresses
The daily and nightly earth; He who refuses
To take failure for an answer till again and again is worn.
Love is waiting for you, waiting for the violence that she chooses
From the tepidity of the common round beyond exhaustion or scorn.
What was once is still and there is no need for remorse;
There are no recriminations in Heaven. O the sensual throb
Of the explosive body, the tumultuous thighs!
Adown a summer lane comes Miss Universe
She whom no lecher's art can rob
Though she is not the virgin who was wise.

The One

Green, blue, yellow and red –
God is down in the swamps and marshes
Sensational as April and almost incred-
      ible the flowering of our catharsis.
A humble scene in a backward place
Where no one important ever looked
The raving flowers looked up in the face
Of the One and the Endless, the Mind that has baulked
The profoundest of mortals. A primrose, a violet,
A violent wild iris – but mostly anonymous performers
Yet an important occasion as the Muse at her toilet
Prepared to inform the local farmers
That beautiful, beautiful, beautiful God
Was breathing His love by a cut-away bog.

October

O leafy yellowness you create for me
A world that was and now is poised above time,
I do not need to puzzle out Eternity
As I walk this arboreal street on the edge of a town.
The breeze too, even the temperature
And pattern of movement is precisely the same
As broke my heart for youth passing. Now I am sure
Of something. Something will be mine wherever I am.
I want to throw myself on the public street without caring
For anything but the prayering that the earth offers.
It is October over all my life and the light is staring
As it caught me once in a plantation by the fox coverts.
A man is ploughing ground for winter wheat
And my nineteen years weigh heavily on my feet.

The Self-Slaved

Me I will throw away.
Me sufficient for the day
The sticky self that clings
Adhesions on the wings.
To love and adventure,
To go on the grand tour
A man must be free
From self-necessity.

See over there
A created splendour
Made by one individual
From things residual
With all the various
Qualities hilarious
Of what
Hitherto was not:

A November mood
As by one man understood;
Familiar, an old custom
Leaves falling, a white frosting
Bringing a sanguine dream
A new beginning with an old theme.

Throw away thy sloth
Self, carry off my wrath
With its self-righteous
Satirizing blotches.
No self, no self-exposure
The weakness of the proser
But undefeatable
By means of the beatable.

I will have love, have love
From anything made of
And a life with a shapely form
With gaiety and charm
And capable of receiving
With grace the grace of living
And wild moments too
Self when freed from you.
Prometheus calls me on.
Prometheus calls me: Son,
We'll both go off together
In this delightful weather.

Canal Bank Walk

Leafy-with-love banks and the green waters of the canal
Pouring redemption for me, that I do
The will of God, wallow in the habitual, the banal,
Grow with nature again as before I grew.
The bright stick trapped, the breeze adding a third
Party to the couple kissing on an old seat,
And a bird gathering materials for the nest for the Word
Eloquently new and abandoned to its delirious beat.
O unworn world enrapture me, encapture me in a web
Of fabulous grass and eternal voices by a beech,
Feed the gaping need of my senses, give me ad lib
To pray unselfconsciously with overflowing speech
For this soul needs to be honoured with a new dress woven
From green and blue things and arguments that cannot be proven.

Our Lady's Tumbler

My verse though light I hope is not
A trivial thing facetious or
Inclined to doggerel at times.
I come to you with verse's chimes
For Easter's sake when tulip time
In Stephen's Green is yours and mine;
Once more, deck chairs and all the knowledge
That's learned in summer's sunny college,
The grass to lie on by the gate
Where we can see down Grafton Street
And get to know new blades of grass
Particular personal visions as
You last year on the Grand Canal
Got to know the mystical
View of Leeson Bridge, the view
That happened to no one else but you.

I come to you to verse my thanks
To parks and flowers and canal banks
I bring you this verse interlude
Our Lady's Tumbler's gratitude.

Question to Life

Surely you would not ask me to have known
Only the passion of primrose banks in May
Which are merely a point of departure for the play
And yearning poignancy when on their own.
Yet when all is said and done a considerable
Portion of living is found in inanimate
Nature, and a man need not feel miserable
If fate should have decided on this plan of it.
Then there is always the passing gift of affection
Tossed from the windows of high charity
In the office girl and civil servant section
And these are no despisable commodity.
So be reposed and praise, praise, praise
The way it happened and the way it is.

The Great Hunger: Introduction

The Great Hunger is Patrick Kavanagh's single most famous poem and it marks a critical juncture in his poetic and personal journey. It is his monumental work and is fashioned from the poet's own experience as a small farmer, together with observations on the lives of his Inniskeen neighbours. In its play of memory and imagination it brings to life a rural world which contrasts with an idealised description of Irish peasant life as contented, simple and uninterruptedly God-centred. It gives the lie to the idyllic and romantic model of life on the land, close to nature, in tune with the seasons and permanently captivated by the wonders of creation and supported by an network of close family and communal ties shedding warmth and humour on a wise and tolerant neighbourly world (cf. section XIII). *The Great Hunger* confronts this comforting, but deceptive, myth. It is a socially, culturally and religiously subversive document which jolts the conventional assumptions and pieties of its time. Writing about his native surroundings, Kavanagh assails the then widely accepted version of life in the Irish countryside. Kavanagh's assault on the rural Catholic idyll was written in Dublin in 1941, in the light of his newly garnered experiences drawn from what seemed to him to be the liberating ethos of metropolitan life which he had come lately to inhabit. He wrote with realism of his country milieu, as he saw it, with telling accuracy and with a disturbing sensibility. The poem's message is a poignant indictment of the dreary purposeless and deprived life of the Irish subsistence farmer of the 1940s, from whom marriage was all too often withheld by reason of domestic and economic circumstances and who was condemned to endure a famished emotional existence for want of normal sexual comforts in womanly companionships. For Kavanagh, this particular denial was the nodal problem which marked the absence of true social stimulation, less still any form of real fulfilment.

The poem is a work of 759 lines divided into 14 sections. Its central character is one Patrick Maguire. Maguire first appears as a distant figure among other farm workers, gathering potatoes in a hilly field in

October. Soon he comes into sharper focus as we are brought close up to this old farmer, outwardly assured, yet inwardly troubled by uncertainties and regrets and consumed with resentment towards those forces responsible for his unhappiness. These antipathies ultimately revolve around three poles which act as constricting symbols. These are identified as three commanding female images: the earth, the mother and the church, each illustrated by the following lines:

… the man who made a field his bride …

O the grip, O the grip of irregular fields …

but the peasant in his little acres is tied, to a mother's womb by the wind-toughened naval …

Religion, the fields and the fear of the Lord

And ignorance giving him the coward's blow …

Maguire's agricultural bondage is compounded by the tyranny of his forceful mother and the influence of the church's teaching. His intellectual energy, like his physical stamina, is drained by the clayey soil to which he has given his life. Confinement to his small fields and his mother's suffocating Catholic mores, aided and abetted by the church, he discerns as the root and cause of the emotional retardation that has stultified his manhood.

The Great Hunger is as original in its form and technique as it is unprecedented in its message. Patrick Maguire's story is told by way of a lengthy flashback that extends from the second to the thirteenth of the poem's sections. There is a cinematic quality to the scenes which it depicts, cutting from indoors to outdoors and from one episode to another. The narrative of Maguire's life proceeds at two levels: the observable doings of the central character, often vividly caught by careful detail, and his inner thoughts, which are supplied by the poet himself as commentator.

The text of the poem may be surveyed under three headings: first, Maguire's story as it is told, secondly, what this tells in its specifically religious perspective, and thirdly, its significance as representing a stage in Kavanagh's poetic journey.

The story told

The poem's narrative covers some thirty years of Patrick Maguire's life retrospectively from age thirty-five to the present which reveals a puzzled and frustrated old man on his way to his seventieth birthday. He regrets the course of his hapless life as he has been condemned to live it. Yet wanly he consoles himself by his efforts at making for himself some slivers of virtue out of necessity: 'He helped a poor woman whose cow Had died on her' … 'He dragged home a drunken man on a winter's night'. Yet the fundamental bitter question prevails throughout: 'is there anything we can prove Of life as it is broken-backed over the Book Of Death?'

> Like a goat tethered to the stump of a tree –
> He circles around and around wondering why it should be.
> No crash,
> No drama.
> That was how his life happened.
> No mad horses galloping in the sky,
> But the weak-washy way of true tragedy …

In the macabre theatre of Maguire's humdrum life as it trails before us, we meet a variegated *dramatis personae* who wind in and out of the story as the seasons and the years pass: his mother, his sister, his priest, his fellow workmen, his neighbours at the crossroad sessions, his card-playing companions, the pub and the church. The narrative is peopled by particular men, women, boys, girls, children, animals, birds, plants and flowers. The reader is made aware not only of Maguire's doings and sayings but also of the private ruminations of his unconscious self, his hopes and fears, as we travel with him over his fields and roam in his company through public and private events in his parish. The poem is comprehensive in its social and emotional vistas. Ironically, the bachelor Maguire is reminded of his sterile existence on every side, by contrast with the fertile landscape where flowers blossom with the seasons, where crops grow repeatedly on the land and animals continually engender offspring. 'The cows and horses breed And the potato-seed

Gives a bud …' But for Maguire and those like him, trapped in a relentless and arid curriculum, 'Life dried in the veins of these women and men: The grey and grief and unlove.'

Maguire is haunted by the procrastinations in his past and the multitude of forever lost aspirations. He had vaguely hoped that the dreary 'circle [of his life] would break down And he would curve the new one to his own will. A new rhythm is a new life …' But 'A year passed and another hurried after it' and the fated farmer is still driven 'back to the growing crops And the ridges he never loved'. This bind reflects Kavanagh's own malaise which caused the postponement of his break from his home at Inniskeen with all its personal restrictions. Maguire, it seems, has lost the struggle for a life that was ample, precious and meaningful although, as the story unfolds, he is revealed as a figure of stoic dignity who compensates for his impoverishment by homely diversions and the primitive satisfactions offered by his fields which, however he may grudge the exertions they entail, still hold him in thrall. In the course of the poem we are given glimpses of oases of pleasure and hope in the midst of his dreary existence. He devises his own emotional escape hatches and scratches some self-esteem from the walls of his world of clay.

The image and symbol of clay with which the poem opens and ends furnishes its primal setting. It suggests a paradox-flavoured work sprung from the earth: dark, unshapen and unpromising, yet elemental, enduring and prolific.

The Great Hunger *in its religious perspective*

Both direct and oblique religious references are found throughout the poem. Kavanagh makes a series of intriguing forays into the domain of Christian belief and practice. These are frequently arresting, infiltrating the narrative with their intuitive power, and thus enriching the text with a distinctly religious complexion. The writer Antoinette Quinn, in her biography of Patrick Kavanagh, is led to declare: '*The Great Hunger* is a Christian critique of a supposedly Christian country.'

Throughout the poem there occur singular observations and queries about God, Jesus Christ and the Catholic Church, which emerge from the poet's own 'point of view' and are stamped with an originality of thought that continues to resound within the reservoir of the Christian imagination. In *The Great Hunger* religious content can be traced in one guise or another in 13 of the 14 sections of the poem. In some passages this is explicit; in others the religious thrust is cloaked in sociocultural commentary.

Explication of the classical compound of the Christian way of life may serve to set the religious scene within which Patrick Kavanagh lived and wrote. This includes three distinct but interwoven strands which together engage the total human person.

Firstly, there is a body of belief which is offered by the story of Jesus Christ and the tradition that flows from the gospels, which has been developed over time by the continuous and universal teaching and witness of the church. This aspect of the Christian way is cogitated by the mind in the light of the gift of faith and forms the credal or doctrinal dimension of Christianity.

Secondly, there is the worshipping and prayerful aspect of the Christian life which invites the believer to share with the community, or privately, in a positive acknowledgement of God in his or her life. The reality and presence of God is encountered in the revelation of the gospels and in the expression of the tradition. In this way the community exercises and energises its faith endowment, which each appropriates to one's self, according to individual abilities, opportunities and religious temperament and which takes place above all in sacramental celebration. This constitutes the liturgical dimension of the Christian enterprise.

Thirdly, there are the moral implications of the Christian teaching which one professes. These address the ethical or behavioural responses that faith proposes and are accomplished by living as generously as possible in accordance with the moral standards entailed by the teaching of the New Testament. For the Christian, these ethical imperatives are illuminated, guided and nourished by attention to God's word, sharing in sacrament and honouring one's neighbour.

All these three components of the Christian life are predicated on the acceptance of a personal God whose real, though of course empirically unverifiable, relationship with human kind is apprehended in terms of what is described as 'unconditional love'. Consequently, in the Christian vision, that faith nexus in turn endows every human being without exception with inalienable personal value. This is the foundational mindset of the classical Christian *persona*. Sustaining and cherishing this three-fold complex of both cognitive and conative aspects of faith in a balance of mutuality constitute the hallmark of Christian identity.

Although Patrick Kavanagh himself would be the last to formally analyse his Catholic matrix in this fashion, yet it was all subliminally present in his lived experience and, consciously or unconsciously, it formed part of his inherited spiritual equipment. It was the entire Christian scheme which supplied him with the background from which issued Kavanagh's religious questions and concerns. It is worth noting that in *The Great Hunger* the religious issues which surface touch on each and all of the Christian categories outlined above. First come the religious passages in the poem which focus on the moral dimension of Christian life. The prevailing version of Catholic moral teaching he indicts repeatedly as a perversion of that 'certain standard, measured and known By which a man might re-make his soul' (cf. VII). Interestingly, however, Kavanagh's strictures on the oppressive sexual ethic of his time and place are situated within the wider doctrinal context of the mysteries of creation and incarnation, references to which recur throughout the poem.

The governing values of creation and the incarnation are subtly and ironically smuggled into the very first lines of *The Great Hunger*. It begins with a dark play on the opening of St John's gospel. The original scriptural lines in question are verses 1 and 14 from its Prologue which read: 'In the beginning was the Word' (the creative Word of God) … 'And the Word was made flesh and dwelt among us' (the incarnation event). By a conflation of these two separate lines of the gospel,

Kavanagh offers his own subversive recension of the text. He writes 'Clay is the word and clay is the flesh', by which he deftly stamps his lines with an unmistakable hint of bathos. This, in effect, empties the gospel text of its pristine power and beauty and conveys to the reader that the biblical revelation has been devalued by the impoverished version of the mysteries of creation and incarnation which are propounded by his church and its priests. Both the wondrous handiwork of the God of creation and the Christ who dignified all flesh through the incarnation are, for him, demeaned and even denied by the insensitivity to nature's miracles and the puritanical, anti-sex, religious mind-set championed by the Catholic culture of his rural society. This atmospheric proclamation in the opening lines of the poem acts as a keynote to the entire, long poem which follows. Within it are to be found strong sentiments of disavowal directed at his inherited religious tradition, but relieved by segments of acceptance of the mystery which God poses through the apparent demands of his revelation. This would seem to reflect the tension that persists at the heart of Kavanagh's personal testament.

Passages of religious protest and disaffection
Possibilities of delights and satisfaction which nature, in Kavanagh's view, was designed to yield, are somehow blocked out and meanly withheld from him. All too seldom is he bestowed 'the narrow slice of divine instruction' which should be available to him in his life at every hand's turn.

> The peasant ploughman who is half a vegetable –
> Who can react to sun and rain and sometimes even
> Regret that the Maker of Light had not touched him more intensely …
> …
> He dare not rise to pluck the fantasies
> From the fruited Tree of Life. He bowed his head
> And saw a wet weed twined about his toe.

Maguire's perplexity urges contradictions with which he wilfully conspires.

He gloried in the lie:
He made it read the way it should,
He made life read, the evil good
While he cursed the ascetic brotherhood
Without knowing why.

The reader is assailed by the emotional power of the protagonist's sombre soul-search, as Maguire puzzles out his lot and destiny.

But the sense of sexual deprivation becomes his obsessive theme.

But his passion became a plague
For he grew feeble bringing the vague
Women of his mind to lust nearness,
Once a week at least flesh must make an appearance.

His frustration drives him even vaguely to entertain the stark surrogate of farm animals to help assuage his forever unrequited erotic instincts. 'He was helpless, he saw his cattle and stroked their flanks in lieu of a wife to handle.' There is a pervasive, primitive, sexual alertness evident throughout the poem. The farming routines are invested with libidinous undertones: ploughing conjures up a symbol of ravening intercourse while planting seed potatoes alludes to sexual intimacy.

The twisting sod rolls over on her back –
The virgin screams before the irresistible sock.
…
                              They put down
The seeds blindly with sensuous groping fingers
And sensual sleep dreams subtly underground.

Less downright are the episodes in the poem that touch on the conventional boy/girl tensions which, nevertheless, automatically usher in the sense of guilt which in his time Maguire has been taught to associate with all things sexual, however natural and innocent they might be.

Once one day in June when he was walking
Among his cattle in the Yellow Meadow
He met a girl carrying a basket –
And he was then a young and heated fellow.

> Too earnest, too earnest! He rushed beyond the thing
> To the unreal. And he saw Sin
> Written in letters larger than John Bunyan dreamt of.

This is one of no less than twelve references in the poem to the appearance of attractive women or girls, described by Maguire, either in generic terms or identified by name. All such encounters would have been regarded as somehow suspect according to what Kavanagh elsewhere describes as 'the so-called moral code that makes love and life impossible'. This was the target of his anger and frustration. He was forced to submit to such constraints and doomed to inhabit

>   … a metaphysical land
> Where flesh was a thought more spiritual than music
> Among the stars – out of the reach of the peasant's hand.

Maguire's moral horizon offers little to light his way:

> In the gap there's a bush weighted with boulders like morality,
> The fools of life bleed if they climb over.

The shadow of the church's expulsion of all blessings of the flesh is cast across the landscape of the poem. This cultural distortion links for the poet with the very project of the incarnation itself. In the Christian understanding of the mystery, all human flesh is redeemed and thereby rendered good, beautiful and even holy. Through the humanity of Jesus 'in whom' for Christians 'the fullness of the Godhead dwells' (Col 2:9-10), every single exchange conducted through the five senses is radically enhanced. One meets the all-spiritual God on the common ground of flesh, his flesh and ours.

The sexual hunger resulting from an over-restrictive moral code is matched by the oppressive liturgical regime illustrated by the atmosphere of his parish church and the baneful influence that emanated from inside its walls. Parishioners are made to feel 'The chapel pressing its low ceiling over them'. Maguire is instructed:

> 'Now go to Mass and pray and confess your sins
> And you'll have all the luck,' his mother said.

Even while working in the fields, liturgical images flitting through his imagination compound his dejection:

> Maguire watches the drills flattened out
> And the flints that lit a candle for him on a June altar
> Flameless.

In the last section of the poem, as Maguire anticipates his death, he indulges in a surreal reverie in which he stoically queries the entire purpose of Christian life. He imagines himself dead and wonders what form of consciousness, if any, will survive. In this dreamlike sequence he raises an ultimate, credal question concerning what he has been taught to believe. Maybe there is a mode of existence after mortal life has ended or maybe not:

> Maybe he will be born again, a bird of an angel's conceit
> To sing the gospel of life …
> Will that be? will that be?

he asks,

> Or is the earth right that laughs haw haw
> And does not believe
> In an unearthly law?
> The earth that says:
> Patrick Maguire, the old peasant, can neither be damned nor glori
> fied.

Again and again Kavanagh rails against what has become for him a blighted experience of creation and the incarnation which in his life have been all too grossly misrepresented and disfigured.

Passages of religious insight and affirmation
A close reading of the poem notably reveals that throughout *The Great Hunger* there are, in fact, only four instances in which Kavanagh refers directly to the repressive nature of Catholic moral teaching. These occur once in section VII, twice in section VIII and once in section IX. Yet these relatively few allusions are so subtly placed in the text that the tone of protest against the church's moral attitudes infiltrates the entire work. Notwithstanding the poem's tenor of scepticism and disillusion-

ment, there is a slender but important vein of hope which tugs at the poet's imagination and offers him flashes of redemptive meaning, inklings of an alternative to the pervasive sense of purposelessness and despair which have materialised for Maguire in a fearful sound of surrender, the 'hysterical laughter of the defeated everywhere'. Laced through the poem's lines are a series of positive religious insights. A distinctive strain of genuine Christian concern breaks the surface of the narrative which serves to nuance his recurrent regret: 'O God, if I had been wiser.' Over against the troughs of dejection, we detect his religious sensibility at work *pari passu,* thus establishing a dialectic between Maguire's spiritual emptiness and a mysterious, dormant religious instinct that is never quite obliterated. At times this emerges in the form of arresting and fresh perceptions which relieve the bleakness of his spiritual landscape. This side of his soul appears, it may be noted, in terms of each of the three dimensions of the Christian scheme mentioned above: doctrinal, liturgical and moral.

As Maguire kneels and prays at Mass, he confesses a moment of hope, confiding to us that in the power of the eucharist and the redemptive worldview which it imparts 'heaven dazzled death'. He continues:

> The congregation lifted its head
> As one man and coughed in unison:
> Five hundred hearts were hungry for life –
> Who lives in Christ shall never die the death
> And the candle-lit Altar and the flowers
> And the pregnant Tabernacle lifted a moment to Prophecy
> Out of the clayey hours.

The Mass-going congregation in the parish embraces persons of every shade of aptitude and acumen. Acknowledging this wide variety of souls, Maguire reminds himself of the consoling reality that 'Christ will meet them at the end of the world, the slow and speedier.'

We have seen that Kavanagh's quarrel with the Catholic Church of his time centred on its life-denying bias which notoriously expressed itself in severe sexual taboos. This had become an emblem of the social and religious culture of his time which he construed as nothing less than a denial of that celebration of redeemed human flesh grounded in material reality that the incarnation signified for him. In this, incidentally, he was in the best of company from the classical, Christian tradition, including the early fathers of the church. He would have approved of the likes of St John Damascene (676-754 AD) who, for example, had declared: 'I worship the creator of matter who became matter for my sake, and who willed to take his abode in matter, who worked out my salvation through matter.'

Kavanagh expostulates:

Religion could not be a counter-irritant like a blister,
But the certain standard measured and known
By which a man might re-make his soul though all walls were down
And all earth's pedestalled gods thrown.

Religion ought to be in essence a positive rather than a negative force and influence in life, providing a flawless message, encouraging us to co-operate with God, as he leads our humanity on its journey towards wholeness. The true purpose of the Catholic religion is to mediate the work of redemption, thus helping us to be healed and established in our own self-worth. This is effected through a process of deliverance and the re-making of ourselves by divine inducement. The work of the 'new creation' must not be forced upon us, but embraced in freedom. But it is forever thwarted by all forms of idolatry, of power and every manner of institutional supremacy. The above lines of the poem are offered, moreover, not as a Kavanagh hypothesis, but rather as a proclamation of what he knows to be true. As such they resound with a particular strength and sureness.

In a mellow passage Maguire considers the possibility of some human fulfilment in this life (cf. section XI). He alludes to the coming of Christ into the world, in a line reminiscent of St Luke's description of the incarnation, as 'a light to those in darkness'. (cf Luke 1:79) Maybe this event will, after all, provide him with the graced resource that will sustain him spiritually. He is inclined to prescribe for himself a more benign outlook on life and a measure of resignation to his lot. Tentatively, he urges:

Let us be kind, let us be kind and sympathetic:
Maybe life is not for joking or for finding happiness in –
This tiny light in Oriental Darkness
Looking out chance windows of poetry or prayer.
And the grief and defeat of men like these peasants
Is God's way – maybe – and we must not want too much
To see.
The twisted thread is stronger than the wind-swept fleece.
And in the end who shall rest in truth's high peace?
Or whose is the world now, even now?
O let us kneel where the blind ploughman kneels
And learn to live without despairing …

In the same section Maguire immediately proceeds to recall how he has, on occasion, behaved in a kindly and tolerant way. He lists generous acts from his past towards unfortunate neighbours, the memory of which lifts his spirit. This short, private meditation ends on a note of pathos:

He saw the sunlight and begrudged no man
His share of what the miserly soil and soul
Gives in a season to a ploughman.
And he cried for his own loss one late night on the pillow
And yet thanked the God who had arranged these things.

By way of postscript to this passage Maguire adds, with coy humour:

Was he then a saint?
A Matt Talbot of Monaghan?

Intimations of God's presence in nature and in the innocent joys of life serve always as a mainstay of Kavanagh's credo. On occasion, it is in the fields that Maguire's religious imagination finds unexpected nourishment. In section III of the poem comes the singular passage in which the reader is made privy to a moment out of doors in which God vividly

re-enacts in nature the foundational Christian mysteries of the Trinity
and the resurrection of the Lord, a delicate epiphany shared among
local neighbours:

> Yet sometimes when the sun comes through a gap
> These men know God the Father in a tree:
> The Holy Spirit is the rising sap,
> And Christ will be the green leaves that will come
> At Easter from the sealed and guarded tomb.

Patrick Kavanagh learned in his youth from the O'Reilly Catechism
that 'God is everywhere' and this basic truth was embedded in his
memory. It would be expressed in his poetry in a multitude of different but convergent forms, shaped by his exceptional religious imagination. Section VI of *The Great Hunger* furnishes us with a sophisticated
religious insight concerning the presence of God in the world. The
poet distinguishes between God's uncreated spirit in the universe and
his localised presence in sacramental form in the Christian Eucharist.
Once enchanted by watching children at play, Maguire records the
scene which leads to a subtle spiritual reflection:

> Picking up a primrose here and a daisy there –
> They were picking up life's truth singly. But he dreamt of the
> > Absolute envased bouquet –
> All or nothing. And it was nothing. For God is not all
> In one place, complete and labelled like a case in a railway store
> Till Hope comes in and takes it on his shoulder –
> O Christ, that is what you have done for us:
> In a crumb of bread the whole mystery is.
>
> He read the symbol too sharply and turned
> From the five simple doors of sense
> To the door whose combination lock has puzzled
> Philosopher and priest and common dunce.
>
> Men build their heavens as they build their circles
> Of friends. God is in the bits and pieces of Everyday –

A kiss here and a laugh again, and sometimes tears,
A pearl necklace round the neck of poverty.

The poet comments in the middle stanza on Maguire's reading of the 'symbol too sharply'. This refers to the contemporary emphasis on the eucharist which encouraged the popular perception of the reserved sacrament as being virtually the sole presence of God among his people. This may be read as a critique on Kavanagh's part of the dualism which obtained in the religious teaching of his day when 'holiness' and reverence for God's presence were associated exclusively with 'in church' occasions – Mass attendance and formal devotional activity, outside of which spirituality hardly existed. The larger truth, however, asserted by the lines that immediately precede and follow this stanza, is that the gift of God's presence is available in all manner of discrete experiences of beauty, friendship and celebration. Nor does the absence of evident material and social well-being exclude God's beneficence or Christ's comfort. The understanding of God's presence, surrounding us in nature and in our relationships with each other, fills in the fuller picture of his love everywhere accessible.

The poem winds to an end not without a note of *double entendre:*

The curtain falls –
Applause, applause.

In one sense this is the sardonic signal of the hero's defeat. It is the end. But, equally, it may also be applause for his survival. Maguire has kept his end up, has somehow been able to withstand the negative, destructive forces with which he has been forced to contend. In short, he has lived to tell his tale.

What The Great Hunger *represents as a stage in Patrick Kavanagh's poetic journey*

Finally, the question arises as to where the poem fits into Patrick Kavanagh's evolving poetic scheme. What is its status in relation to the poet's final and fully matured vision and his enduring legacy? The substance and quality of the work are indisputable. It may be recalled what

The Great Hunger set out to achieve – to dismantle the social and religious assumptions which held sway in Kavanagh's rural society of the 1930s and 1940s. In its autobiographical intent, it deals grimly and candidly, through the medium of the poem's central character, with a particular time and place. The picture of life which the poem paints is, by and large, a scene of social and spiritual desolation. Patrick Maguire is a figure on the edge of despair. He decries the oppressive family arrangements which plague his spirit and he doubts even the entire *raison d'être* of the religious system which he experienced as a form of enslavement. There is no one and nothing he can trust: not a god to whom he hardly relates in any intelligible, not to say loving, manner and whom he can only fear and resent. Nor can he trust life itself nor even his own heart and soul. All is suspect except, perhaps, in a curious way, his own fields and the passage of time itself: 'perennial grass' and 'only time can bless'.

Maguire's life is deprived emotionally, intellectually and spiritually. A bitter irony of *The Great Hunger* stems from an intimation on his part of a shocking self-deception that began in boyhood and can end only with his death. For all of this, the poem marks a pivotal moment in Kavanagh's development and serves as a catalyst in his personal outlook which led to the shaping of his later poetry of repose and the forging of what, in time, became known as his 'comic vision' of life. Through the monumental work of *The Great Hunger*, Patrick Kavanagh may be said to have expurgated the anger, distress and frustration that had beset him and which are symbolised in the misfortunes of the poem's tragic figure of Patrick Maguire. In spite of the wounds inflicted on his character by church, family and his agrarian society, it seems, nevertheless, that the poem's protagonist has come through his marathon and stressful experience of living, with a residual spiritual sensitivity still intact, as well as retaining a healthy respect for the land and all that it stood for. Maguire survives, it appears, in spite of the church but also, paradoxically, because of it. It was the church which furnished a major segment of the materiality, so to speak, of his experience. Its heavy-handed presence was the force with which he had to contend. It was the reality, ever present and provocative, that confronted him, the quarry on which his sights were trained and which triggered his broadsides against its function and credentials. Intimations of spiritual substance and promise, however, continue to peep through chinks in his moral armour. Maguire's outdoor, workaday routines admitted 'half moments of paradise' complemented indoors in church by 'the candle-lit Altar [which] lifted a moment to Prophecy'. Ironically, it was the Christian revelation, however perversely presented, that fanned his appetite for the Spirit. In his imaginative campaign of resistance, Maguire fashions for himself a stubborn buoyancy by which he manages, just barely, to keep afloat. In *The Great Hunger* Kavanagh interrogates and excoriates the religious system of his day. He was called to deal with this obstacle and deal with it he did, in his own way. It was necessary for him to write *The Great Hunger,* but in his own good time he had to leave it behind and move on, but not without bequeathing it to us for our sober instruction. The poem is a documentary work marking the direction that his quest for identity had taken. It is an affirmation of his belief that the surest way to self-understanding and unity of being lay through honest and realistic writing about his environment as he perceived it.

The Great Hunger was written in 1941. Some three years later Kavanagh himself began to have misgivings about aspects of his long, landmark poem. He sensed that the doctrinaire antagonisms of the work were at variance with his evolving preference for a less tendentious style of writing. He had moved to a new and essentially inward poetic demeanour, which he was to describe as an attitude of 'not caring' and which drove him towards a non-judgmentalism in his approach that was, as we know, to produce a more insouciant poetic *persona.* The narrator's voice in *The Great Hunger* he subsequently deemed to be excessively rhetorical and so *parti pris* as to eclipse at times the credibility of the poem's central character. Kavanagh recognised that the voice behind Maguire was tainted by its ideological persistence. The 'preacher's voice' was no longer appropriate. Kavanagh's ambition would be to aspire to what he called a quality of 'gaiety', reposing his newly found poetic faith more in the joyously irrational, while developing a strong bent towards the activity of praise and celebration in his work. Eventually Patrick Kavanagh actually repudiated *The Great Hunger*. This decision was consistent with his matured credo and was, it seems, inevitable. In his *Self Portrait* in 1962 Kavanagh was to say: 'There are some queer and terrible things in *The Great Hunger* but it lacks the nobility and repose of poetry.' In his preface to the *Collected Poems* in 1964 he wrote: '*The Great Hunger* is concerned with the woes of the poor. A true poet is selfish and implacable. A poet merely states the position and does not care whether his words change anything or not.' Kavanagh grew to believe that sociological concern formed no part of the true poet's brief and this view ties with his emergent 'comic' vision which was to become the poet's literary lodestar. 'There is only one Muse,' he insisted, 'the Comic Muse. In tragedy there is always something of a lie. Great poetry is always comic, in the profound sense. Comedy is abundance of life.' 'Tragedy,' he continues, 'is under-developed comedy, not fully born. Had I stuck to the tragic thing in *The Great Hunger* I would have found many powerful friends … but I lost my messianic compulsion. I sat on the bank of the Grand Canal in the summer of 1955 and let the waters lap idly on the shores of my mind. My purpose in life was to have no purpose.' Kavanagh's thinking had made a quantum leap from dire depths to a dramatically higher flight path, considerably more lightsome in character. Kavanagh's change of *Zeitgeist* within three short years is illustrated by two contrasting quotations, which echo each other, but in a sense are in attitudinal opposition. The last lines of *The Great Hunger* (1941) read:

The bedposts fall. No hope. No. No lust.

The hungry fiend

Screams the apocalypse of clay

In every corner of this land.

And towards the end of another poem, *A Wreath for Thomas Moore's Statue** (1944), he writes:

But hope! the poet comes again to build
A new city high above lust and logic,
The trucks of language overflow and magic
At every turn of the living road is spilled.

In assessing any poet's published work, orthodoxy demands that the literary critic has no interest whatsoever in the private personality of the poet in question. His personal views, beliefs and lifestyle are officially irrelevant to the task. The firm principle that holds in this respect is that the text and the text alone speaks. However, since the specifically religious content of the poetry of Patrick Kavanagh is the formal object of this enquiry, literary questions, as such, do not arise. For this reason a pastoral aspect of all that Kavanagh represents becomes a legitimate interest. The question follows, therefore: how does the Christian content of so much of Kavanagh's poetry relate to the religious ideas and attitudes of the man himself? What teaching on the life of the Spirit is to be mined from his prophetic utterance in *The Great Hunger*? What is to be learned from the total Kavanagh, from his poetry as it appears on the page and his personal 'point of view' which continuously informed his writing? Clues for our enlightenment emerge from Patrick Kavanagh's biographer, Antoinette Quinn. She captures something of the contradictory, yet focused, drift of his thoughts and emotions as he confronts the mystery of God and how he appropriates to himself his Catholic faith and its tradition. She writes of his 'quite complicated attitude towards Catholicism: a compound of belief and scepticism, affectionate tolerance and fierce criticism, superstitious fear and, as in *The Great Hunger*, the imaginative and intellectual power to conceive of an alternative to the popular Irish conception of a prudent and sexually prudish Deity, a God who always says yes. While he deplored the religious absolutism of Patrick Maguire, waiting to be presented with "the Absolute envased bouquet" instead of contenting himself with the ordinary wild flowers that came his way, he himself was sometimes such an idealist that even God himself could hardly be godly enough for him. One or other of this mix of attitudes might be in the ascendant at different times, though throughout the 1940s and 1950s he continued to be a practising Catholic, regularly attending Sunday Mass in St Mary's Church at Haddington Road or, sometimes, the Sacred Heart Church in Donnybrook.' 'From 1942,' Antoinette Quinn asserts, 'Catholicism would be integral to Kavanagh's literary radicalism.' (*Patrick Kavanagh*, pp. 192-3)

The dark, religious vexation which dominated the case history of Patrick Maguire's soul was in time transcended by his poetic creator.

The Great Hunger remains for us not only a literary *tour de force* but also a reproachful social benchmark for which all of an older generation of Irish men and women must somehow take responsibility. It continues to occupy an important niche in the canon of both our literature and our history.

The Great Hunger

I

Clay is the word and clay is the flesh
Where the potato-gatherers like mechanised scare-crows move
Along the side-fall of the hill – Maguire and his men.
If we watch them an hour is there anything we can prove
Of life as it is broken-backed over the Book
Of Death? Here crows gabble over worms and frogs
And the gulls like old newspapers are blown clear of the hedges, luckily.
Is there some light of imagination in these wet clods?
Or why do we stand here shivering?
                    Which of these men
Loved the light and the queen
Too long virgin? Yesterday was summer. Who was it
    promised marriage to himself
Before apples were hung from the ceilings for Hallowe'en?
We will wait and watch the tragedy to the last curtain
Till the last soul passively like a bag of wet clay
Rolls down the side of the hill, diverted by the angles
Where the plough missed or a spade stands, straitening the way.

A dog lying on a torn jacket under a heeled-up cart,
A horse nosing along the posied headland, trailing
A rusty plough. Three heads hanging between wide-apart
Legs. October playing a symphony on a slack wire paling.
Maguire watches the drills flattened out
And the flints that lit a candle for him on a June altar
Flameless. The drills slipped by and the days slipped by
And he trembled his head away and ran free from the world's halter,
And thought himself wiser than any man in the townland
When he laughed over pints of porter
Of how he came free from every net spread

In the gaps of experience. He shook a knowing head
And pretended to his soul
That children are tedious in hurrying fields of April
Where men are spanging across wide furrows.
Lost in the passion that never needs a wife –
The pricks that pricked were the pointed pins of harrows.
Children scream so loud that the crows could bring
The seed of an acre away with crow-rude jeers.
Patrick Maguire, he called his dog and he flung a stone in the air
And hallooed the birds away that were the birds of the years.

Turn over the weedy clods and tease out the tangled skeins.
What is he looking for there?
He thinks it is a potato, but we know better
Than his mud-gloved fingers probe in this insensitive hair.

'Move forward the basket and balance it steady
In this hollow. Pull down the shafts of that cart, Joe,
And straddle the horse,' Maguire calls.
'The wind's over Brannagan's, now that means rain.
Graip up some withered stalks and see that no potato falls
Over the tail-board going down the ruckety pass –
And *that's* a job we'll have to do in December,
Gravel it and build a kerb on the bog-side. Is that Cassidy's ass
Out in my clover? Curse o' God –
Where is that dog?
Never where he's wanted.' Maguire grunts and spits
Through a clay-wattled moustache and stares about him from the
    height.
His dream changes again like the cloud-swung wind
And he is not so sure now if his mother was right
When she praised the man who made a field his bride.

Watch him, watch him, that man on a hill whose spirit
Is a wet sack flapping about the knees of time.
He lives that his little fields may stay fertile when his own body
Is spread in the bottom of a ditch under two coulters crossed in
    Christ's Name.

He was suspicious in his youth as a rat near strange bread
When girls laughed; when they screamed he knew that meant
The cry of fillies in season. He could not walk
The easy road to his destiny. He dreamt
The innocence of young brambles to hooked treachery.
O the grip, O the grip of irregular fields! No man escapes.
It could not be that back of the hills love was free
And ditches straight.
No monster hand lifted up children and put down apes
As here.
              'O God if I had been wiser!'
That was his sigh like the brown breeze in the thistles.
He looks towards his house and haggard. 'O God if I had been wiser!'
But now a crumpled leaf from the whitethorn bushes
Darts like a frightened robin, and the fence
Shows the green of after-grass through a little window,
And he knows that his own heart is calling his mother a liar.
God's truth is life – even the grotesque shapes of his foulest fire.

The horse lifts its head and cranes
Through the whins and stones
To lip late passion in the crawling clover.
In the gap there's a bush weighted with boulders like morality,
The fools of life bleed if they climb over.

The wind leans from Brady's, and the coltsfoot leaves are holed with
    rust,
Rain fills the cart-tracks and the sole-plate grooves;
A yellow sun reflects in Donaghmoyne
The poignant light in puddles shaped by hooves.

Come with me, Imagination, into this iron house
And we will watch from the doorway the years run back,
And we will know what a peasant's left hand wrote on the page,
Be easy, October. No cackle hen, horse neigh, tree sough, duck quack.

II

Maguire was faithful to death:
He stayed with his mother till she died
At the age of ninety-one.
She stayed too long,
Wife and mother in one.
When she died
The knuckle-bones were cutting the skin of her son's backside
And he was sixty-five.

O he loved his mother
Above all others.
O he loved his ploughs
And he loved his cows
And his happiest dream
Was to clean his arse
With perennial grass
On the bank of some summer stream;
To smoke his pipe
In a sheltered gripe
In the middle of July –
His face in a mist

And two stones in his fist
And an impotent worm on his thigh.

But his passion became a plague
For he grew feeble bringing the vague
Women of his mind to lust nearness,
Once a week at least flesh must make an appearance.

So Maguire got tired
Of the no-target gun fired
And returned to his headlands of carrots and cabbage
To the fields once again
Where eunuchs can be men
And life is more lousy than savage.

III

Poor Paddy Maguire, a fourteen-hour day
He worked for years. It was he that lit the fire
And boiled the kettle and gave the cows their hay.
His mother tall hard as a Protestant spire
Came down the stairs bare-foot at the kettle-call
And talked to her son sharply: 'Did you let
The hens out, you?' She had a venomous drawl
And a wizened face like moth-eaten leatherette.
Two black cats peeped between the banisters
And gloated over the bacon-fizzling pan.
Outside the window showed tin canisters.
The snipe of Dawn fell like a whirring noise
And Patrick on a headland stood alone.

The pull is on the traces, it is March
And a cold black wind is blowing from Dundalk.
The twisting sod rolls over on her back –
The virgin screams before the irresistible sock.

No worry on Maguire's mind this day
Except that he forgot to bring his matches.
'Hop back there Polly, hoy back, woa, wae,'
From every second hill a neighbour watches
With all the sharpened interest of rivalry.
Yet sometimes when the sun comes through a gap
These men know God the Father in a tree:
The Holy Spirit is the rising sap,
And Christ will be the green leaves that will come
At Easter from the sealed and guarded tomb.

Primroses and the unearthly start of ferns
Among the blackthorn shadows in the ditch,
A dead sparrow and an old waistcoat. Maguire learns
As the horses turn slowly round the which is which
Of love and fear and things half born to mind.
He stands between the plough-handles and he sees
At the end of a long furrow his name signed
Among the poets, prostitute's. With all miseries
He is one. Here with the unfortunate
Who for half moments of paradise
Pay out good days and wait and wait
For sunlight-woven cloaks. O to be wise
As Respectability that knows the price of all things
And marks God's truth in pounds and pence and farthings.

IV
April, and no one able to calculate
How far is it to harvest. They put down
The seeds blindly with sensuous groping fingers,
And sensual sleep dreams subtly underground.
Tomorrow is Wednesday – who cares?
'Remember Eileen Farrelly? I was thinking

A man might do a damned sight worse …' That voice is blown
Through a hole in a garden wall –
And who was Eileen now cannot be known.

The cattle are out on grass,
The corn is coming up evenly.
The farm folk are hurrying to catch Mass:
Christ will meet them at the end of the world, the slow and speedier.
But the fields say: only Time can bless.

Maguire knelt beside a pillar where he could spit
Without being seen. He turned an old prayer round:
'Jesus, Mary and Joseph pray for us
Now and at the Hour.' Heaven dazzled death.
'Wonder should I cross-plough that turnip-ground.'
The tension broke. The congregation lifted its head
As one man and coughed in unison.
Five hundred hearts were hungry for life –
Who lives in Christ shall never die the death.
And the candle-lit Altar and the flowers
And the pregnant Tabernacle lifted a moment to Prophecy
Out of the clayey hours.
Maguire sprinkled his face with holy water
As the congregation stood up for the Last Gospel.
He rubbed the dust off his knees with his palm, and then
Coughed the prayer phlegm up from his throat and sighed: Amen.

Once one day in June when he was walking
Among his cattle in the Yellow Meadow
He met a girl carrying a basket –
And he was then a young and heated fellow.
Too earnest, too earnest! He rushed beyond the thing
To the unreal. And he saw Sin

Written in letters larger than John Bunyan dreamt of.
For the strangled impulse there is no redemption.
And that girl was gone and he was counting
The dangers in the fields where love ranted.
He was helpless. He saw his cattle
And stroked their flanks in lieu of wife to handle.
He would have changed the circle if he could,
The circle that was the grass track where he ran.
Twenty times a day he ran round the field
And still there was no winning post where the runner is cheered home.
Desperately he broke the tune,
But however he tried always the same melody crept up from the
    background,
The dragging step of a ploughman going home through the guttery
Headlands under an April-watery moon.
Religion, the fields and the fear of the Lord
And Ignorance giving him the coward's blow
He dare not rise to pluck the fantasies
From the fruited Tree of Life. He bowed his head
And saw a wet weed twined about his toe.

                    V
Evening at the cross-roads –
Heavy heads nodding out words as wise
As the rumination of cows after milking.
From the ragged road surface a boy picks up
A piece of gravel and stares at it – and then
He flings it across the elm tree on to the railway.
It means nothing,
Not a damn thing.
Somebody is coming over the metal railway bridge
And his hobnailed boots on the arches sound like a gong
Calling men awake. But the bridge is too narrow –

The men lift their heads a moment. That was only John,
So they dream on.

Night in the elms, night in the grass.
O we are too tired to go home yet. Two cyclists pass
Talking loudly of Kitty and Molly –
Horses or women? wisdom or folly?

A door closes on an evicted dog
Where prayers begin in Barney Meegan's kitchen;
Rosie curses the cat between her devotions;
The daughter prays that she may have three wishes –
Health and wealth and love –
From the fairy who is faith or hope or compounds of.

At the cross-roads the crowd had thinned out:
Last words are uttered. There is no tomorrow;
No future but only time stretched for the mowing of the hay
Or putting an axle in the turf-barrow.

Patrick Maguire went home and made cocoa
And broke a chunk off the loaf of wheaten bread;
His mother called down to him to look again
And make sure that the hen-house was locked. His sister grunted in
    bed
The sound of a sow taking up a new position.
Pat opened his trousers wide over the ashes
And dreamt himself to lewd sleepiness.
The clock ticked on. Time passes.

VI

Health and wealth and love he too dreamed of in May
As he sat on the railway slope and watched the children of the place
Picking up a primrose here and a daisy there –
They were picking up life's truth singly. But he dreamt of the
    Absolute envased bouquet –
All or nothing. And it was nothing. For God is not all
In one place, complete and labelled like a case in a railway store
Till Hope comes in and takes it on his shoulder –
O Christ, that is what you have done for us:
In a crumb of bread the whole mystery is.

He read the symbol too sharply and turned
From the five simple doors of sense
To the door whose combination lock has puzzled
Philosopher and priest and common dunce.

Men build their heavens as they build their circles
Of friends. God is in the bits and pieces of Everyday –
A kiss here and a laugh again, and sometimes tears,
A pearl necklace round the neck of poverty.

He sat on the railway slope and watched the evening,
Too beautifully perfect to use,
And his three wishes were three stones too sharp to sit on,
Too hard to carve. Three frozen idols of a speechless muse.

VII

'Now go to Mass and pray and confess your sins
And you'll have all the luck,' his mother said.
He listened to the lie that is a woman's screen
Around a conscience when soft thighs are spread.
And all the while she was setting up the lie

She trusted in Nature that never deceives.
But her son took it as the literal truth.
Religion's walls expand to the push of nature. Morality yields
To sense – but not in little tillage fields.

Life went on like that. One summer morning
Again through a hay-field on her way to the shop –
The grass was wet and over-leaned the path –
And Agnes held her skirts sensationally up,
And not because the grass was wet either.
A man was watching her, Patrick Maguire.
She was in love with passion and its weakness
And the wet grass could never cool the fire
That radiated from her unwanted womb
In that country, in that metaphysical land
Where flesh was a thought more spiritual than music
Among the stars – out of the reach of the peasant's hand.

Ah, but the priest was one of the people too –
A farmer's son – and surely he knew
The needs of a brother and sister.
Religion could not be a counter-irritant like a blister
But the certain standard measured and known
By which a man might re-make his soul though all walls were down
And all earth's pedestalled gods thrown.

VIII
Sitting on a wooden gate,
Sitting on a wooden gate,
Sitting on a wooden gate
He didn't care a damn.
Said whatever came into his head,
Said whatever came into his head,

Said whatever came into his head
And inconsequently sang.
Inconsequently sang
While his world withered away,
He had a cigarette to smoke and a pound to spend
On drink the next Saturday.
His cattle were fat
And his horses all that
Midsummer grass could make them.
The young women ran wild
And dreamed of a child.
Joy dreams though the fathers might forsake them
But no one would take them,
No one would take them;
No man could ever see
That their skirts had loosed buttons,
Deliberately loosed buttons.
O the men were as blind as could be.
And Patrick Maguire
From his purgatory fire
Called the gods of the Christian to prove
That this twisted skein
Was the necessary pain
And not the rope that was strangling true love.

But sitting on a wooden gate
Sometime in July
When he was thirty-four or five
He gloried in the lie:
He made it read the way it should,
He made life read the evil good
While he cursed the ascetic brotherhood
Without knowing why.
Sitting on a wooden gate

All, all alone
He sang and laughed
Like a man quite daft,
Or like a man on a channel raft
He fantasied forth his groan.
Sitting on a wooden gate,
Sitting on a wooden gate,
Sitting on a wooden gate
He rode in day-dream cars.
He locked his body with his knees
When the gate swung too much in the breeze.
But while he caught high ecstasies
Life slipped between the bars.

IX

He gave himself another year,
Something was bound to happen before then –
The circle would break down
And he would curve the new one to his own will.
A new rhythm is a new life
And in it marriage is hung and money.
He would be a new man walking through unbroken meadows
Of dawn in the year of One.

The poor peasant talking to himself in a stable door –
An ignorant peasant deep in dung.
What can the passers-by think otherwise?
Where is his silver bowl of knowledge hung?
Why should men be asked to believe in a soul
That is only the mark of a hoof in guttery gaps?
A man is what is written on the label.
And the passing world stares but no one stops
To look closer. So back to the growing crops

And the ridges he never loved.
Nobody will ever know how much tortured poetry the pulled weeds
    on the ridge wrote
Before they withered in the July sun,
Nobody will ever read the wild, sprawling, scrawling mad woman's
    signature,
The hysteria and the boredom of the enclosed nun of his thought.
Like the afterbirth of a cow stretched on a branch in the wind
Life dried in the veins of these women and men:
The grey and grief and unlove,
The bones in the backs of their hands,
And the chapel pressing its low ceiling over them.

Sometimes they did laugh and see the sunlight,
A narrow slice of divine instruction.
Going along the river at the bend of Sunday
The trout played in the pools encouragement
To jump in love though death bait the hook.
And there would be girls sitting on the grass banks of lanes
Stretch-legged and lingering staring –
A man might take one of them if he had the courage.
But 'No' was in every sentence of their story
Except when the public-house came in and shouted its piece.

The yellow buttercups and the bluebells among the whin bushes
On rocks in the middle of ploughing
Was a bright spoke in the wheel
Of the peasant's mill.
The goldfinches on the railway paling were worth looking at –
A man might imagine then
Himself in Brazil and these birds the Birds of Paradise
And the Amazon and the romance traced on the school map lived
    again.

Talk in evening corners and under trees
Was like an old book found in a king's tomb.
The children gathered round like students and listened
And some of the saga defied the draught in the open tomb
And was not blown.

X

Their intellectual life consisted in reading
Reynolds' News or the *Sunday Dispatch*
With sometimes an old almanac brought down from the ceiling
Or a school reader brown with the droppings of thatch.
The sporting results or the headlines or war
Was a humbug profound as the highbrow's Arcana.
Pat tried to be wise to the abstraction of all that
But its secret dribbled down his waistcoat like a drink from a strainer.
He wagered a bob each way on the Derby,
He got a straight tip from a man in a shop –
A double from the Guineas it was and thought himself
A master mathematician when one of them came up
And he could explain how much he'd have drawn
On the double if the second leg had followed the first.
He was betting on form and breeding, he claimed,
And the man that did that could never be burst.
After that they went on to the war, and the generals
On both sides were shown to be stupid as hell.
If he'd taken *that* road, they remarked of a Marshal,
He'd have … O they know their geography well.
This was their university. Maguire was an undergraduate
Who dreamed from his lowly position of rising
To a professorship like Larry McKenna or Duffy
Or the pig-gelder Nallon whose knowledge was amazing.
'A treble, full multiple odds … That's flat porter …
My turnips are destroyed with the blackguardly crows …

Another one … No, you're wrong about that thing I was telling you …
Did you part with your filly, Jack? I heard that you sold her …'
The students were all savants by the time of pub-close.

XI

A year passed and another hurried after it
And Patrick Maguire was still six months behind life –
His mother six months ahead of it;
His sister straddle-legged across it: –
One leg in hell and the other in heaven
And between the purgatory of middle-aged virginity –
She prayed for release to heaven or hell.
His mother's voice grew thinner like a rust-worn knife
But it cut more venomously as it thinned,
It cut him up the middle till he became more woman than man,
And it cut through to his mind before the end.

Another field whitened in the April air
And the harrows rattled over the seed.
He gathered the loose stones off the ridges carefully
And grumbled to his men to hurry. He looked like a man who could
    give advice
To foolish young fellows. He was forty-seven,
And there was depth in his jaw and his voice was the voice of a great
    cattle-dealer,
A man with whom the fair-green gods break even.
'I think I ploughed that lea the proper depth,
She ought to give a crop if any land gives …
Drive slower with the foal-mare, Joe.'
Joe, a young man of imagined wives,
Smiled to himself and answered like a slave:
'You needn't fear or fret.
I'm taking her as easy, as easy as …
Easy there Fanny, easy pet.'

They loaded the day-scoured implements on the cart
As the shadows of poplars crookened the furrows.
It was the evening, evening. Patrick was forgetting to be lonely
As he used to be in Aprils long ago.
It was the menopause, the misery-pause.

The schoolgirls passed his house laughing every morning
And sometimes they spoke to him familiarly –
He had an idea. Schoolgirls of thirteen
Would see no political intrigue in an old man's friendship.
Love
The heifer waiting to be nosed by the old bull.
That notion passed too – there was the danger of talk
And jails are narrower than the five-sod ridge
And colder than the black hills facing Armagh in February.
He sinned over the warm ashes again and his crime
The law's long arm could not serve with 'time'.

His face set like an old judge's pose:
Respectability and righteousness,
Stand for no nonsense.
The priest from the altar called Patrick Maguire's name
To hold the collecting box in the chapel door
During all the Sundays of May.
His neighbours envied him his holy rise,
But he walked down from the church with affected indifference
And took the measure of heaven angle-wise.

He still could laugh and sing,
But not the wild laugh or the abandoned harmony now
That called the world to new silliness from the top of a wooden gate
When thirty-five could take the sparrow's bow.
Let us be kind, let us be kind and sympathetic:
Maybe life is not for joking or for finding happiness in –

This tiny light in Oriental Darkness
Looking out chance windows of poetry or prayer.
And the grief and defeat of men like these peasants
Is God's way – maybe – and we must not want too much
To see.
The twisted thread is stronger than the wind-swept fleece.
And in the end who shall rest in truth's high peace?
Or whose is the world now, even now?
O let us kneel where the blind ploughman kneels
And learn to live without despairing
In a mud-walled space–
Illiterate, unknown and unknowing.
Let us kneel where he kneels
And feel what he feels.

One day he saw a daisy and he thought it
Reminded him of his childhood –
He stopped his cart to look at it.
Was there a fairy hiding behind it?

He helped a poor woman whose cow
Had died on her;
He dragged home a drunken man on a winter's night;
And one rare moment he heard the young people playing on the
   railway stile
And he wished them happiness and whatever they most desired from
   life.

He saw the sunlight and begrudged no man
His share of what the miserly soil and soul
Gives in a season to a ploughman.
And he cried for his own loss one late night on the pillow
And yet thanked the God who had arranged these things.

Was he then a saint?
A Matt Talbot of Monaghan?

His sister Mary Anne spat poison at the children
Who sometimes came to the door selling raffle tickets
For holy funds.
'Get out you little tramps!' she would scream
As she shook to the hens an apronful of crumbs,
But Patrick often put his hand deep down
In his trouser-pocket and fingered out a penny
Or maybe a tobacco-stained caramel.
'You're soft,' said the sister; 'with other people's money
It's not a bit funny.'

The cards are shuffled and the deck
Laid flat for cutting – Tom Malone
Cut for trump. I think we'll make
This game, the last, a tanner one.
Hearts. Right. I see you're breaking
Your two-year-old. Play quick, Maguire,
The clock there says it['s] half-past ten –
Kate, throw another sod on that fire.
One of the card-players laughs and spits
Into the flame across a shoulder.
Outside, a noise like a rat
Among the hen-roosts. The cock crows over
The frosted townland of the night.
Eleven o'clock and still the game
Goes on and the players seem to be
Drunk in an Orient opium den.
Midnight, one o'clock, two.
Somebody's leg has fallen asleep.
What about home? Maguire are you

Using your double-tree this week?
Why? do you want it? Play the ace.
There's it, and that's the last card for me.
A wonderful night, we had. Duffy's place
Is very convenient. Is that a ghost or a tree?
And so they go home with dragging feet
And their voices rumble like laden carts.
And they are happy as the dead or sleeping …
I should have led that ace of hearts.

XII
The fields were bleached white,
The wooden tubs full of water
Were white in the winds
That blew through Brannagan's Gap on their way from Siberia;
The cows on the grassless heights
Followed the hay that had wings –
The February fodder that hung itself on the black branches
Of the hilltop hedge.
A man stood beside a potato-pit
And clapped his arms
And pranced on the crisp roots
And shouted to warm himself.
Then he buck-leaped about the potatoes
And scooped them into a basket.
He looked like a bucking suck-calf
Whose spine was being tickled.
Sometimes he stared across the bogs
And sometimes he straightened his back and vaguely whistled
A tune that weakened his spirit
And saddened his terrier dog's.
A neighbour passed with a spade on his shoulder
And Patrick Maguire bent like a bridge

Whistled – good morning under his oxter,
And the man the other side of the hedge
Champed his spade on the road at his toes
And talked an old sentimentality
While the wind blew under his clothes.

The mother sickened and stayed in bed all day,
Her head hardly dented the pillow, so light and thin it had worn,
But she still enquired after the household affairs.
She held the strings of her children's Punch and Judy
    and when a mouth opened
It was her truth that the dolls would have spoken
If they hadn't been made of wood and tin –
'Did you open the barn door, Pat, to let the young calves in?'
The priest called to see her every Saturday
And she told him her troubles and fears:
'If Mary Anne was settled I'd die in peace –
I'm getting on in years.'
'You were a good woman,' said the priest,
'And your children will miss you when you're gone.
The likes of you this parish never knew,
I'm sure they'll not forget the work you've done.'
She reached five bony crooks under the tick –
'Five pounds for Masses – won't you say them quick.'
She died one morning in the beginning of May
And a shower of sparrow-notes was the litany for her dying.
The holy water was sprinkled on the bed-clothes
And her children stood around the bed and cried because it was too
    late for crying.
A mother dead! The tired sentiment:
'Mother mother' was a shallow pool
Where sorrow hardly could wash its feet …
Mary Anne came away from the deathbed and boiled the calves their
    gruel.

O what was I doing when the procession passed?
Where was I looking?
Young women and men
And I might have joined them.
Who bent the coin of my destiny
That it stuck in the slot?
I remember a night we walked
Through the moon of Donaghmoyne,
Four of us seeking adventure –
It was midsummer forty years ago.
Now I know
The moment that gave the turn to my life.
O Christ! I am locked in a stable with pigs and cows for ever.

XIII

The world looks on
And talks of the peasant:
The peasant has no worries;
In his little lyrical fields
He ploughs and sows;
He eats fresh food,
He loves fresh women,
He is his own master
As it was in the Beginning
The simpleness of peasant life.
The birds that sing for him are eternal choirs,
Everywhere he walks there are flowers.
His heart is pure,
His mind is clear,
He can talk to God as Moses and Isaiah talked –
The peasant who is only one remove from the beasts he drives.
The travellers stop their cars to gape over the green bank into his
    fields: –

There is the source from which all cultures rise,
And all religions,
There is the pool in which the poet dips
And the musician.
Without the peasant base civilization must die,
Unless the clay is in the mouth the singer's singing is useless.
The travellers touch the roots of the grass and feel renewed
When they grasp the steering wheels again.
The peasant is the unspoiled child of Prophecy,
The peasant is all virtues – let us salute him without irony
The peasant ploughman who is half a vegetable –
Who can react to sun and rain and sometimes even
Regret that the Maker of Light had not touched him more intensely.
Brought him up from the sub-soil to an existence
Of conscious joy. He was not born blind.
He is not always blind: Sometimes the cataract yields
To sudden stone-falling or the desire to breed.

The girls pass along the roads
And he can remember what man is,
But there is nothing he can do.
Is there nothing he can do?
Is there no escape?
No escape, no escape.

The cows and horses breed,
And the potato-seed
Gives a bud and a root and rots
In the good mother's way with her sons;
The fledged bird is thrown
From the nest – on its own.
But the peasant in his little acres is tied
To a mother's womb by the wind-toughened navel-cord

Like a goat tethered to the stump of a tree –
He circles around and around wondering why it should be.
No crash,
No drama.
That was how his life happened.
No mad hooves galloping in the sky,
But the weak, washy way of true tragedy –
A sick horse nosing around the meadow for a clean place to die.

XIV

We may come out into the October reality, Imagination,
The sleety wind no longer slants to the black hill where Maguire
And his men are now collecting the scattered harness and baskets.
The dog sitting on a wisp of dry stalks
Watches them through the shadows.
'Back in, back in.' One talks to the horse as to a brother.
Maguire himself is patting a potato-pit against the weather –
An old man fondling a new-piled grave:
'Joe, I hope you didn't forget to hide the spade,
For there's rogues in the townland. Hide it flat in a furrow.
I think we ought to be finished by tomorrow.'
Their voices through the darkness sound like voices from a cave,
A dull thudding far away, futile, feeble, far away,
First cousins to the ghosts of the townland.

A light stands in a window. Mary Anne
Has the table set and the tea-pot waiting in the ashes.
She goes to the door and listens and then she calls
From the top of the haggard-wall:
'What's keeping you
And the cows to be milked and all the other work there's to do?'
'All right, all right,
We'll not stay here all night.'

Applause, applause,
The curtain falls.
Applause, applause
From the homing carts and the trees
And the bawling cows at the gates.
From the screeching water-hens
And the mill-race heavy with the Lammas floods curving over the weir.
A train at the station blowing off steam
And the hysterical laughter of the defeated everywhere.
Night, and the futile cards are shuffled again.
Maguire spreads his legs over the impotent cinders that wake no
    manhood now
And he hardly looks to see which card is trump.
His sister tightens her legs and her lips and frizzles up
Like the wick of an oil-less lamp.
The curtain falls –
Applause, applause.

Maguire is not afraid of death, the Church will light him a candle
To see his way through the vaults and he'll understand the
Quality of the clay that dribbles over his coffin.
He'll know the names of the roots that climb down to tickle his feet.
And he will feel no different than when he walked through
    Donaghmoyne.
If he stretches out a hand – a wet clod,
If he opens his nostrils – a dungy smell;
If he opens his eyes once in a million years –
Through a crack in the crust of the earth he may see a face nodding in
Or a woman's legs. Shut them again for that sight is sin.

He will hardly remember that life happened to him –
Something was brighter a moment. Somebody sang in the distance.
A procession passed down a mesmerized street.

He remembers names like Easter and Christmas
By the colour his fields were.
Maybe he will be born again, a bird of an angel's conceit
To sing the gospel of life
To a music as flightily tangent
As a tune on an oboe.
And the serious look of the fields will have changed to the leer of a
    hobo
Swaggering celestially home to his three wishes granted.
Will that be? will that be?
Or is the earth right that laughs: haw haw
And does not believe
In an unearthly law.
The earth that says:
Patrick Maguire, the old peasant, can neither be damned nor glorified:
The graveyard in which he will lie will be just a deep-drilled potato-
    field
Where the seed gets no chance to come through
To the fun of the sun.
The tongue in his mouth is the root of a yew.
Silence, silence. The story is done.

He stands in the doorway of his house
A ragged sculpture of the wind,
October creaks the rotted mattress,
The bedposts fall. No hope. No. No lust.
The hungry fiend
Screams the apocalypse of clay
In every corner of this land.

Lough Derg: Introduction

The tradition of pilgrimage is deeply rooted in the Catholic soul. For that matter, it is also to be found, in some shape or form, in all the great religions of the world. Historically, the Jewish people looked to Jerusalem and its temple as a magnetic place of holiness towards which they were beckoned on pilgrimage. The Muslim obligation of the Hadj to Mecca is well-known to all, and the Hindu religion has its own sacred venues on which great numbers converge on special occasions. The practice of pilgrimage, it seems, is part of a primal religious instinct.

For those acquainted with Irish Catholic faith and culture, Lough Derg, where what is known as St Patrick's Purgatory is situated, has been and still is a familiar destination, either through personal experience or, at least, by hearsay. In the light of this it is not surprising that Patrick Kavanagh turned his mind to this extraordinary pilgrimage and eventually made it the subject of a long poem. He would have been conversant with the remarkable antiquity of Lough Derg and its unusual place in Ireland's Christian history. Growing up in Monaghan, his imagination must have been stirred by local folklore concerning the pilgrimage and the fascination that it held for the people of his time. Its location, as it happens, actually fell within the confines of his native diocese of Clogher. Kavanagh visited Lough Derg for the first time in 1940, returning again in 1942, after which he set about dealing with the pilgrimage in poetic form. For one reason or another, his eponymous poem was not published in his lifetime. It was to appear for the first time eleven years after his death, in 1978.

There is a sense in which *Lough Derg* is a referential commentary on the entire history of Catholicism in Ireland. Symbolically it extends beyond a particular place and experience to cover the larger religious story of a people. It reflects a national faith tradition, with its tribulations and triumphs and with its religious vicissitudes, marked alternatively by fragility and sturdiness. It spans the centuries from

Christianity's Patrician beginnings, through the Middle Ages, the Reformation and enduring, extraordinarily, down to our own day. The Lough Derg narrative represents the intertwining of the spiritual, social, cultural and political strands that have combined to forge the Hiberno-Catholic identity: the religious idiosyncrasies of early Celtic Christianity with its penitential texture, the extravagance of European, medieval theological conceits, the repressive face of English land-lordism, the ecclesiastical assertiveness of post-emancipation Irish Catholicism and the latter-day quest for spirituality, now ambiguously emerging in our time.

In *The Penguin Book of Irish Verse,* its editor, Professor Brendan Kennelly, includes the poem *Lough Derg* as his chosen specimen of Kavanagh's work, presenting it even as a paradigm of the equivocal traits of the Irish soul. Of it, he writes: 'The far-reaching consequences of Kavanagh's confrontation of the full spiritual range of Irish life, from grovelling squalor to unconscious magnanimity, have yet to be realised. *Lough Derg* is a monumental example of the energy and courage that mark that confrontation. Like all Kavanagh's best work, *Lough Derg* goes beyond satire and savage criticism to reach its truest tone, his unique music, that of instinctive celebratory revelation.' (p. 42)

The unique nature of the pilgrimage and its durability in Catholic life are summarised by Kavanagh himself in the poem:

Lough Derg, St Patrick's Purgatory in Donegal,
Christendom's purge. Heretical
Around the edges: the centre's hard
As the commonsense of a flamboyant bard.
The twentieth century blows across it now
But deeply it has kept an ancient vow.

The rituals of the modern Lough Derg pilgrimage and their proven-ance may seem curious to the uninitiated. Its rubrics, extending over the three days and three nights of the island's exercises, are linked to practices which have evolved over centuries. Without some explanation of the Lough Derg story, the modern-day event remains a matter of some mystification to the outsider. Since the Spartan, spiritual routines of the pilgrimage's 'desert' experience, with its vigil, fasting and prayer formulae, feature prominently throughout the poem, some knowledge of the historical background to the pilgrimage itself is desirable. Otherwise Kavanagh's poetic narrative remains, in many respects, less than fully intelligible. For that reason, an outline of the antecedents of today's Lough Derg serves to contextualise the poem and may be a helpful preparation towards embarking on the 643 lines of the work itself.

The story of Lough Derg and its pilgrimage

First, an explanation of the three different titles associated with the place and the event: Lough Derg, St Patrick's Purgatory and Station Island.

Lough Derg: One possible derivation of the word 'Derg' to describe the lake itself comes from the old Irish word *derc* meaning an eye which came to describe an apparture or hole in the ground. This would correspond to the pit or cave which was the focal point of the penitential exercise until 1780 when it was replaced by a chapel. A simpler and perhaps more plausible derivation of Derg is from the Irish word *dearg* meaning red. This would refer to the somewhat russet coloured waters of the lake, caused by minerals in the mainland soil surrounding Lough Derg.

St Patrick's Purgatory: The association of the name of St Patrick with Lough Derg goes back to earliest times. There is some evidence that Patrick travelled in its vicinity which was conducive to solitude and prayer by reason of its remote location and bleak terrain. The term 'purgatory' in the title tells of the practice of early pilgrims being immured in the famous cave which became for them a figure of purgatory during their statutory twenty-four hours of darkness and deprivation therein. This was construed as a period of expiatory suffering in repentance for their sins.

Station Island: The term 'station', from the Latin *statio,* meant a penitential stopping place, as in the Station Churches during the Lenten liturgy of Rome. On Lough Derg the word 'station' is used to denote a complex pattern of prayer recited around the circles of low stone walls known as 'beds'. Going 'on station' refers to the pilgrimage as a whole.

Originally a monastic foundation existed from the fifth century on the lake at Saints' Island. However, since the twelfth century, the smaller, neighbouring Station Island has been the renowned centre of pilgrimage. Interestingly, St Patrick's Purgatory was the most prominent landmark on several maps of Ireland drawn during the Renaissance period. With the opening up of the Irish church to European influences in the twelfth century, the pilgrimage became singularly famous across the continent, rivalling other leading medieval shrines abroad. Pilgrims travelled to the Irish island from different parts of Europe, including Spain, Holland, England, Germany and Hungary and various other countries. St Patrick's Purgatory became such a well-known placename that it was alluded to in one form or another by numerous outstanding religious and literary figures from the European past. It is mentioned, for example, by St Catherine of Siena, the celebrated printer Caxton and Geraldus Cambrensis. Its European, literary pedigree includes references to be found in Shakespeare's *Hamlet* and Ariosto's *Orlando Furioso*. Dante was aware of St Patrick's Purgatory as he wrote his *Divine Comedy* with its purgatorial passages. In modern times Lough Derg has also been the subject of a substantial poem by the Irish poet Denis Devlin and, subsequent to Kavanagh's poem, a volume of Seamus Heaney's, entitled *Station Island,* once more returns for inspiration to the Donegal sanctuary. In prose, Sean O'Faolain's accomplished short story *Lovers of the Lake* celebrates the pilgrimage. Apart from literature, two unusual imprints, so to speak, of Lough Derg are to be seen today in Italy: the deep, subterranean well of St Patrick at Orvieto and a striking fourteenth-century fresco at Todi in Umbria, featuring the purgatorial cave on Lough Derg's Station Island.

By far the most famous Lough Derg manuscript is the account in Latin of one Knight Owein who visited the Island c. 1180 and of which

150 copies survive in libraries throughout Europe. It is, in addition, the source of very many later vernacular versions of his island pilgrimage story. This work became something of an extensive 'bestseller' in the twelfth century and thus exerted an important influence on the European mind of its time. The widespread fascination with Owein's tale of St Patrick's Purgatory coincided with a distinctive medieval religious development which was a preoccupation with purgatory as a state or place of ongoing purification in the next world. In the popular mind, purgatory became a remotely situated halfway house which the intrepid pilgrim might explore. The medieval worldview easily embraced the belief that the next world was equally as real as the present world, if indeed not more so. Questions as to the nature of the world beyond were a constant source of curiosity. Owein's tale told how he spent fifteen days in prayer and fasting before being admitted to the purgatorial pit or cavern on the island, fearing he might never return from his ordeal. On entering, he experienced visions of tormented souls and was assailed by demonic forces. Undergoing severe tortures with the dire prospect of being doomed forever, he invokes the name of Jesus, the Saviour, which enables him to pass safely over a bridge that crossed the entrance to hell, eventually entering a paradise of beauty and joy. Thus he survives and, re-emerging from the cave twenty-four hours later, spends fifteen further days in prayerful thanksgiving for his safe deliverance. To the people of his time, Owein's fabulous account, with its elements of chivalry and daring, its location in Ireland at the edge of the known world, a kind of interface between this life and the next – this was a gripping, cautionary tale. Besides, as it happens, it was a faithful acting out of a renowned feature of early Irish pilgrimage, known always as the *eachtra* or adventure.

Native Irish notables, including chieftains, poets and other folk, regularly frequented the penitential island down the years. By the beginning of the 1500s, however, the note of *eachtra* or exploit and of visions and marvels connected with the pilgrimage fades and Irish contemporary references make no mention of them nor, indeed, of the

European tales of earlier currency. Though incarceration in the cave remained in vogue, the extensive poetic accounts of later times become sober testimonies to a struggle not with demons but with the hardness of the authors' own unrepentant hearts. For example, there is a seventeenth-century poem ascribed posthumously (following a common literary ploy) to the prestigious thirteenth-century poet Donnachadh Mór Ó Dálaigh (d. 1244). The poem, entitled in English *Sad Is My Pilgrimage to Lough Derg*, confesses: 'In this narrow prison of hard stone, after all I had done of evil and pride: but how pitiful that I cannot shed a tear and I buried alive in a grave.'

The long, domestic history of Lough Derg is both chequered and colourful. One memorable, if bizarre, episode from the twelfth century, in which the pilgrimage accidentally features, concerns the story of the adulterous union of Devorgilla, wife of Tiernan O Rourke of Breffny, with Diarmuid (na nGall) MacMurrough. This fateful elopement occurred, of all times, while Devorgilla's pious husband was absent from home on pilgrimage to the island. This extramarital liaison was so frowned on by the other Irish chieftains that, as a consequence, Diarmuid was ultimately denied the high kingship of Ireland in favour of Rory O'Connor of Connacht. A disappointed Diarmuid went on to usher the Normans into Ireland and the rest, as we know, is history.

Predictably, the Reformation, with its political repercussions in Ireland, eventually brought tribulation for the pilgrimage. In 1596 the family of the notoriously chameleon ecclesiastical figure, Myler McGrath, who had held the Lough Derg territory in trust for the church, passed the property over to English law jurisdiction, still retaining its proprietorship and acquiring an English title in the process. In 1632 the pilgrimage was suppressed and the Anglican Bishop of Clogher, James Spottiswood, personally supervised the destruction of everything on the island. However, despite the hostile measures of Established Church and State combined, the pilgrimage revived and continued subversively. The site was again demolished by the authorities in 1680, but still the pilgrimage somehow survived, defying even a

1704 Act of Parliament which decreed public whipping for anyone who resorted to the penitential island.

The national patrimony of pilgrim records, found in both poetry and prose, stretch across the centuries. Notably a manuscript bequeathed to posterity by Michael O'Clery of The Four Masters (c. 1600) details for the first time the prayers and exercises of the pilgrimage in a form that corresponds with the practices of our own day. William Carleton, who was specially revered by Patrick Kavanagh, made the pilgrimage as a young man and wrote of it in 1828. In view of the long, literary lineage pertaining to the Lough Derg experience, it was, perhaps, inevitable that Patrick Kavanagh was bound to explore what has been a constantly recurring topic in Irish writing.

The Lough Derg pilgrimage remains alive and well in our own times. It is a triduum undertaking: three days of fast, only one snack of dry bread or toast with black tea or coffee or water being taken each day. Pilgrims come to the island fasting from midnight and shed their footwear on arrival. It is remarkable how being barefoot throughout the pilgrimage reduces all to a palpable experience of communal equality which induces a singular camaraderie.

Nine penitential stations are performed over the three days. Each station involves the repeated silent praying of the Lord's Prayer, the Hail Mary and the Apostles' Creed, as pilgrims make their way from the basilica to St Patrick's Cross, St Brigid's Cross, around the basilica outside and then, in order, around the penitential beds or cells. At each bed they pray, walking three times around the outside, kneeling at the entrance, walking around the inside and kneeling at the cross in the centre. Then they pray at the water's edge, return to St Patrick's Cross and thence to the basilica. Three stations are made on the first day of the pilgrimage, the prayers and actions of four more are performed in common within the basilica during the night vigil, one is made outside on the second day and one on the third day.

The Eucharist and Night Prayer are celebrated in common in the basilica on each of the two evenings the pilgrim is on the island. A twenty-four-hour vigil from sleep is observed from 10 p.m. on the first evening, beginning with a reflection on the nature and scope of the pilgrimage and a time of preparation for the sacrament of Reconciliation. This celebration takes place on the second morning and concludes with the renewal of baptismal promises at midday. The struggle to ward off sleep is punctuated by the Way of the Cross in the afternoon and by the evening Eucharist, and bed is more than welcome on the second night of the pilgrim's stay on the island. They leave on the following morning after Mass and having made their final station, but their fast continues until midnight of the third day. The pilgrimage season extends each year from Pentecost Sunday (beginning of June) to the harvest feast of the Assumption of Our Lady on 15 August.

Lough Derg, the poem

Patrick Kavanagh approached the writing of his long poem in an ambiguous frame of mind. It was written, in fact, within weeks of his second visit to the island sanctuary. He had first experienced the pilgrimage two years previously, in 1940. He was despatched by the editor of *The Standard* newspaper to report on the opening of the pilgrimage season on 1 June 1942, and this was his second visit. His subsequent article in *The Standard* reveals Kavanagh's mixed feelings on the island experience. He wrote in *The Standard* then that his 'first and strongest impression' was, interestingly, of the 'freshness and recency of Christianity', 'the excitement of the new truth … stirring the imagination of men and women'. However, he added his quota of negative comment, criticising the apparently unreflective piety of the participants and their over-assured robotic submission to the repetitive exercises of the pilgrimage regime. This critical ambiguity was noteworthy at the time in an avowedly Catholic publication such as *The Standard*. Kavanagh's ambiguity vis-à-vis the Lough Derg pilgrimage is sustained in his poem that was to follow. It could be argued that *Lough Derg* might have benefited by a more marked degree of detachment had Kavanagh not embarked on the work almost immediately after his visit to the island, allowing no time or space for his experience to settle and mature in his mind before the pilgrimage and its symbolism came to be permanently memorialised by him. Be that as it may, the carping note of the opening lines of the poem might also possibly connect with the irritation the poet suffered on the occasion of his previous and first visit to the island in 1940 when he had stood aloof from the other pilgrims waiting to embark for Station Island. On that occasion his attention-seeking posture drew cutting banter on his head from the local boatmen. This humiliation had upset him at the time. It remained hypersensitively with him and continued to colour his association of Lough Derg with what he regarded as both a crew and 'cargo' of hostile unworthies. Thus the poem begins:

> From Cavan and from Leitrim and from Mayo
> From all the thin-faced parishes where hills
> Are perished noses running peaty water,
> They come to Lough Derg to fast and pray and beg
> With all the bitterness of nonentities, and the envy
> Of the inarticulate when dealing with an artist.

The poem oscillates throughout between scorn and sympathy for the pilgrims as Kavanagh tries to strike a balance between the two.

> (O God of Truth,
> Keep him who tells this story straight,
> Let no cheap insincerity shape his mouth).

The poet identifies the various types to be found among his fellow pilgrims. They include the smug, the spiritually warped and the manipulative but also those who are sincere. In the motley island gathering, the whole country of Ireland, north and south, becomes, as it were, one parish for the duration of the pilgrimage. In this perspective Station Island embraces men and women from town and countryside and from twelve of the thirty-two counties of Ireland: laity and clerics, the professional classes, farmers, civil servants and shopkeepers. All sorts of souls foregather at St Patrick's Purgatory. A selection from the large and variegated company is presented close up in the poem which, resembling the technique of *The Great Hunger*, offers a window on the goodness and failings, the hopes and anxieties and the fortunes and woes of the wartime Ireland of the 1940s. Again, as in *The Great Hunger*, the poet-narrator both describes the pilgrimage scenes in cinematic images and also explores the mindsets and interior dispositions of individual pilgrims. There are glimpses of the pilgrims at prayer in the basilica and circulating around the penitential beds, going to confession, battling with the urge to sleep during the all-night vigil, the striking up of chance acquaintances in the vacant hours, the swopping of confidences and even flirtatious exchanges. The slow, sequential order of the pilgrimage events is marked in the narrative, underlining the tedium of the island's penitential endurance test:

And the day crawled lazily
Along the orbit of Purgatory.

The narrator's role is a mixture of observer and pilgrim, outsider and insider. But if in *The Great Hunger* Kavanagh tries to prove too much by his angry attacks on his clearly identified target, the oppressive mores of a rural society and its church, in *Lough Derg* the poet's vacillating attitudes towards the island experience amount to an indeterminate conclusion concerning the pilgrimage experience. He strives throughout the poem to achieve an objectivity in his treatment of the religious culture which Lough Derg so starkly, yet for him in a strange way also so winningly, presents. Yet he wobbles in his task, venting his spleen on some features of the pilgrim population and the entire enterprise, while reining in his prejudices as he is confronted with the spiritual power and purpose generated by the Station Island phenomenon. There is Kavanagh's dismissive 'homicidal' ire:

Said the poet then,
This piety that hangs like a fool's, unthought,
This certainty in men
This three days too-goodness,
Too-neighbourly cries
Temptation to murder
Mediocrities.

Yet there is his profoundly sensed affirmation of Lough Derg:

> But deeply it has kept an ancient vow
> It knows the secret of pain ...

As the poem progresses, one discovers an increasingly positive response towards pilgrimage as a manifestation of faith, building towards a benign, tolerant judgement which just about prevails. However, Kavanagh's concluding confessional pronouncement on his poem seems to leave his intention and achievement somehow unresolved:

> All happened on Lough Derg as it is written
> In June nineteen forty-two
> When the Germans were fighting outside Rostov.
> The poet wrote it down as best he knew
> As integral and completed as the emotion
> Of men and women cloaking a burning emotion
> In the rags of the commonplace, will permit him.
> He too was one of them. He too denied
> The half of him that was his pride
> Yet found it waiting, and the half untrue
> Of this story is his pride's rhythm.

As in the figure of Patrick Maguire in *The Great Hunger,* there is, as one might suspect, a less prominent, but definite autobiographical layer to be detected in *Lough Derg.* In the first of the poem's sub-plots one Robert Fitzsimons is introduced with references to his style and behaviour recurring eight times throughout the narrative. Fitzsimons, 'the red-haired man', is an intellectually pretentious farmer who, despite sustained effort, fails to win a woman, Aggie Meegan, to whom he is attracted. This episode mimics something of Kavanagh's own notoriously unsuccessful amorous techniques. His grandiose attempts to impress women whom he desired mostly proved counterproductive, ending fruitlessly. Perhaps Kavanagh recognised himself in Robert Fitzsimons' frustration? The second and minor sub-plot may also connect with an early Kavanagh misadventure. A Franciscan friar appears who has been suspended from his priestly duties as a result of sexual involvement with a schoolgirl. Does the friar's tale echo Kavanagh's own recorded first sexual encounter with a girl of similarly tender age?

Religious content of the poem

As soon as the poem gets into its stride the poet-commentator adverts to the suspicion of all things beautiful, vibrant and life-enhancing which characterises, according to him, the typical Lough Derg clientele. This spiritual dourness of his fellow citizens was the unappealing perception of the Irish religious disposition, often uppermost in Kavanagh's mind whenever he turned to matters Catholic in his native land. In 1955 he was to write in his own publication, *Kavanagh's Weekly,* that 'somewhere in the nineteenth century' Ireland became infected with 'an anti-life heresy' disseminated by priests trained in Maynooth.

Applying this conviction to the Lough Derg pilgrims, he assumes them to be bereft of all Christian *joie de vivre* and immediately condemns them as simply a sombre life-denying lot:

Their hands push closed the doors that God holds open.

Love sunlit is an enchanter in June's hours

And flowers and lights. These to shopkeepers and small lawyers

Are heresies up beauty's sleeve.

The poem includes references to several Christian themes which become for Kavanagh the source either of passing approval or the provoking of adverse comment.

However, this downbeat verdict is checked later on in the poem, when he comes to recognise a number of worthwhile and even admirable strands to be found in the pilgrims' search for renewed faith and some form of spiritual enlightenment as they set about their island exertions. The poem's narrative, together with commentary on the conduct of the pilgrimage, is wide-ranging. Although Kavanagh's observations stray in numerous directions during the course of the poem, it is possible to comb out from the text a series of topics which accumulate to form a significant body of Catholic belief and practice. Although the poet touches on religious tenets, sometimes in an unusual way and predictably from his very own 'point of view', nevertheless it is possible to extrapolate the doctrines in question with a view to examining them systematically as they surface in the poem.

The elements from the Catholic tradition around which the poem is built are principally six in number, all interrelated. They deal with penance, guilt, forgiveness, prayer, the interplay of the individual and community in the Catholic vision, and the timeless nature of the Christian event.

Penance

And through
The flames of St Patrick's Purgatory
I go offering every stone-bruise, all my hunger;
In the back-room of my penance I am weaving
An inside-shirt for charity.

It is penance which supplies the *raison d'être* of the Lough Derg pilgrimage. In St Mark's gospel, the first recorded words of Jesus in his public ministry read, 'The time has come and the reign of God is near; repent and believe the Good News.' (Mark 1:15) The Greek word *metanoia* is used in the New Testament to express the total interior conversion, the radical change of heart that is involved in Jesus' call to repentance. This disposition of genuine repentance was possible only when one emulated the attitude of a child (Matthew 18:3) and turned away from the conceits of self-righteousness and presumption (Luke 18:10-14). The repentance which Jesus taught was good news to be received with joy. Although he did not prescribe any penitential liturgies, Jesus did require baptism for the forgiveness of sins and a faith in his gospel which would reconcile humanity to God. This Christian truth is echoed in the poem, by the pilgrimage custom of rehearsing part of the sacrament of Christian Initiation in the basilica. 'Our vows of baptism we again take.' This is evoked at the start of every Lough Derg pilgrimage station outside the church, as one moment in the baptismal liturgy is repeated, with outstretched arms, according to the ancient Irish ritual of what was called *Comhrair Chrábuid*:

A queue of pilgrims waiting to renounce
The World, the Flesh, the Devil and all his house.

Repentence remains a part of Christian life, normally to be realised simply through the formal sacrament of penance, and sometimes supplemented by other devotional activity such as pilgrimages and vigils. Because sinfulness in one form or another persists in both individual lives and in the malign structures of society, the call to repentance requires both personal and societal conversion.

The tradition of fasting as a component of penance is especially deeply rooted in Irish Christian memory. In recent times it has come to be practised as a symbol of personal renunciation in favour of deprived or oppressed groups in society. The educated instinct for abstinence as a means of spiritual tuning or sensory refinement may recommend itself independently of any specific religious context. At a strictly physical or psychological level, renunciation of material comforts and satisfactions can work to promote a higher state of wellbeing and effect a liberation of the human spirit. It frequently plays a part in the pursuit of holistic fitness in the realm of sport and athletics. Extravagant regimes of spiritual penance have tended, however, to become tainted with an unhealthy predilection for pain and suffering. Historically, penitential practices have emerged within Christianity which have verged on the masochistic. These can be traced to an old, baneful temptation to spiritual distortion found in the Manichean heresy which regarded the body and all matter as evil. This led to their ruthless subjugation. An integrated Christian outlook will eschew this false dualism, remembering the primitive affirmation in this regard. When God had completed his material creation, he 'saw all that he had made and indeed it was very good'. (Genesis 1:31). Moreover, by virtue of the incarnation, Christians believe that all flesh is radically redeemed.

Our attitude towards all forms of asceticism originates in the teaching and example of Jesus. His approach to penance and fasting is distinctly nuanced. It is at once both world-embracing and world-denying (cf. Matthew 9:14-15). On the one hand, there is the Christian belief in the positive value of creation together with its joyful concomitants. On the other hand, one realistically acknowledges the potential waywardness of the human condition which is ever prone to the abuse of God's blessings. Hence the law of God sometimes requires resistance to one's immediate instincts, in preparation for which occasional voluntary self-denial is demanded. Kavanagh writes in *Lough Derg*:

> For this is the penance of the poor
> Who know what beauty hides in misery
> As beggars, fools and eastern fakirs know.

The phrase 'beauty hides in misery' may be one way of hinting at the wholesome self-mastery and consequent freedom of spirit which accrues from the acceptance of reasonable self-denial. The special knowledge which the poet attributes as a prerogative of the three categories of persons mentioned above may echo a like message rendered by Jesus when he prayed: 'I bless you Father, Lord of Heaven and Earth, for hiding these things from the learned and the clever and revealing them to mere children' (Matthew 11:25).

But one note on these lines may clarify the distinctive nature of Christian renunciation. It differs, it seems, from the commonly understood motivation of 'eastern fakirs', whose feats of abnegation appear principally as an endurance test. For the Christian there is no merit in self-denial for its own sake, but only in so far as it is a work of love pointing to a higher good. Asceticism can never be positively evaluated in physical terms alone. Its genuine power is generated by the spiritual disposition which backs it. Its authenticity springs from its source and purpose which will always be nothing other than confidence in God, just as Jesus' own sufferings and death were entrusted to his and our God. The necessary context of love which validates penance is perhaps suggested in the theological sureness of touch revealed by the Lough Derg pilgrim quoted at the beginning of this section:

> In the back-room of my penance I am weaving
> An inside-shirt for charity. [i.e. love]

Christianity does not seek the liberation of humankind from suffering, but rather its transformation through the death and resurrection of Jesus Christ. Penance without context is meaningless but, in the poet's line, like 'a heap of stones anywhere is consecrated by love's terrible need'.

Kavanagh writes, towards the end of the poem, that Lough Derg 'knows the secret of pain'. He is here suggesting that the faith tradition of St Patrick's Purgatory remains in tune with a profound understanding of how Christian penitential activity, wisely regulated, can be healing, refreshing and offering even an entry to the mystery of redemption itself?

Guilt
    … the old
    Kink in the mind, the fascination
    Of sin troubled the mind of God …

Kavanagh suggests that the excessive preoccupation with sin and guilt among the Lough Derg pilgrims is such an aberration that it disturbs even the mind of God himself. The implication is that the Almighty did not ordain that this should be so.

The experience of guilt in the wake of wrongdoing is part of universal human experience. When genuinely objective guilt is recognised by our conscience it can help us to grow morally and enhance our level of personal responsibility. Thus, an acknowledgement of having offended God or our neighbour helps us to redress the effects of our behaviour when we realise that it transgresses what we know in our heart of hearts is right and good. Without the experience of normal guilt, the hurts we inflict on others will remain unchecked and unhealed. Guilt, however, is never an end in itself but is always the servant of the gifts of repentence, reconciliation and even spiritual renewal. What may be described as feelings of guilt never serve a morally useful purpose and may, indeed, prove to be downright unhealthy. If and when guilt feelings begin to bear little or no relationship to objective reality, they signal a neurotic condition. Kavanagh sees feelings of guilt as attaching particularly to the sexual dimension of Irish life. The centrality of sex as a moral issue has popularly been blamed on the Irish Catholic Church. Although the Judaeo-Christian tradition includes the sixth and ninth commandments, the moral teaching of Jesus Christ extends, of course, to many other areas of human life and behaviour, covering justice, truth, compassion and integrity of life in general. Sexually centred admonitions loom less than large in the teaching of Jesus. Indeed, most famously, his encounter with the woman taken in adultery is distinguished for its non-judgmental approach and sympathetic conclusion. (cf John 7:3-11)

Forgiveness
For here's the day of a poor soul freed
To a marvellous beauty above its head.
The gift of God's forgiveness comes to the pilgrims, according to Kavanagh, as an experience of interior liberation from sin and evil and is construed as something precious conferred on the penitent from a source which is immeasurably more wonderful than any earthly agent. It issues from beyond the limited realm of human authority. The Christian religion believes that God's love for every single human being is inexhaustible and unconditional. We are first loved by him and are invited to respond to this love as best we can. Whenever and however we offend against God, his mercy is forever at hand to forgive us, once we simply acknowledge that we stand in need of the reconciling of our relationship with the One who cannot but cherish us, come what may. The parables of Jesus illustrating the nature of the Christian God disclose him as the source and end of all loving – absolute love itself.

In the Lough Derg poem the pervasive Irish 'fascination of sin' is blamed by Kavanagh on the seventeenth-century Jansenist heresy which is said to have infiltrated the moral teaching of the Irish church, thus injecting it with a guilt-driven momentum. Towards the end of the poem the two aspects of the penitential experience, both the guilt and the forgiveness, are combined by Kavanagh in a brisk, lapidary 19 line passage:

The sharp knife of Jansen
Cuts all the green branches,
Not sunlight comes in
But the hot-iron sin
Branding the shame
Of a beast in the Name
Of Christ on the breast
Of a child of the West.
It was this he had read.
All day he was smitten
By this foul legend written
In the fields, in the skies,
In the sanctuaries.
But now the green tree
Of humanity
Was leafing again
Forgiveness of sin.
A shading hand over
The brow of the lover.

Prayer

The first evening they prayed till nine o'clock
Around the gravel rings, a hundred decades
Of rosaries until they hardly knew what words meant –
Their own names when they spoke them sounded mysterious.

In these lines Kavanagh catches the atmosphere of the island pilgrimage, the penitential movements around the 'beds' as each 'station' is completed, the seemingly endless prayer and the condition of near hypnosis which the strenuous Lough Derg regime induces in the single-minded, intense throng of pilgrims. Prayer, whether spoken aloud or privately recited, forms the continuous *leitmotif* of the entire proceedings. The performance of prayer hallmarks the Christian personality. It is woven through every aspect of the lives of those who are believers in the gospel of Jesus Christ. As such, it is linked with all five of the other headings dealt with in this study.

Prayer provides the life-blood, so to speak, of the Christian community which is understood as nothing less than the body of Christ, socially embodied throughout the world in the visible, corporate reality of the baptised everywhere and in every era. Prayer is the raising of the mind and heart to God, and the duty and invitation to prayer is broadly composed of either, in the first place, expressions of praise of God and thanking him for his goodness or, secondly, what is called prayer of petition, asking God to fulfil our needs while being nourished in our faith, hope and love. It may be practised either by reciting set formulae or by silent contemplation of the mystery of God. Petitionary prayer may, on the face of it, seem unnecessary since God knows all our needs (Matthew 6:8) but it seems that he wills that we present them to him in prayer, not as a demand on our part but as an explicit expression of trust, so that our experience of need becomes part of a personal relationship with God.

The attraction of prayer in the Lough Derg setting is celebrated by Kavanagh when he writes:

Lough Derg in the dawn poured rarer cups. Prayer

And fast that makes the sourest drink rare.

The marked beneficence of prayer is experienced in the poem even by the at first nonchalant 'half-pilgrim' figure of Robert Fitzsimons, 'who hated prayer' but who found that it actually drew him towards an intimacy with the person of Jesus Christ. He had come to Lough Derg

to please the superstition

Which says, 'At least the thing can do no harm'

Yet he alone went out with Jesus fishing.

In the practice of prayer, Christians follow the example of Jesus himself who prayed frequently to God the Father as recorded in the gospels (cf Mark 1:9-11, 9:2-8, 14:36, John 17:1-26). The classical Christian prayer suggested by Jesus to his followers is, of course, the Our Father which comprises both praise and petition. The Eucharist is, in fact, the summit of Christian prayer. The word itself means thanksgiving and this memorial or ritual re-enactment of God's manifestation of supreme love for us, and the believers' appreciative response, constitute the apogee of Christian prayer. It could be said, moreover, that prayer even governs what followers of Jesus profess in faith, in view of the primitive axiom of the church which declares that 'the law of prayer is the law of belief'.

The orthodox pattern of classical Christian prayer which is founded on faith, hope and love, is that believers relate to God the Father, in Jesus Christ, through the Holy Spirit.

In the poem Kavanagh devotes all of 80 lines to describing the detailed prayers of petition framed partly in a litanical format by five different pilgrims: a mother and farmer's wife, a would-be husband, a young girl from Castleblayney, an unemployed young man and an older man who sets his 'will in Communion and Confession' but who, nevertheless, continually falls back into sinful ways 'in spite of penance, prayer and canticle'.

By detailing the prayer petitions of the pilgrims, the poet penetrates their inmost thoughts and discovers the homely, human needs that beset each of them in turn.

Significantly Kavanagh's verdict on this outpouring of devotion is clearly positive. Regarding the 'Beggary that God heard', the poet asks:

Was he bored
As men are with the poor? Christ Lord
Hears in the voices of the meanly poor
Homeric utterances, poetry sweeping through.

These ordinary, undistinguished petitioners, who might simply bore the 'worldly wise', enjoy a dignity and stature in God's sight, each one being singly known and uniquely loved by him. Echoing the minutiae of God's providence, as expressed in the gospels of both Mark and Luke, he makes his point more dramatically with the lines:

Only God thinks of the dying sparrow
In the middle of a war. (cf Mark 10:29; Luke 12:6)

Kavanagh endows these humble prayers with the poetic status of 'odes and sonnets' which, for him, is the highest praise he can offer. He even extravagantly invokes the immortal lines of the *Odyssey* and the *Iliad* of Homer in reference to these 'deep prayers'. In this he places them on a pinnacle of esteem.

The interplay between the individual and the community in the Christian vision

A man's the centre of the world,
A man is not an anonymous
Member of the general public.
The Communion of Saints
Is a Communion of individuals.
God the Father is the Father
Of each one of us.

In the above passage Kavanagh reaffirms his profound belief in the unique value of the individual in the Christian tradition. In this he is professing a foundational truth which is not only paramount in theological terms but which has over the centuries filtered through the Catholic tradition into the political philosophy of Western Europe and which, it might be argued, underpins the democratic structures of our parliamentary democracies. It is historically clear that the best features of Christendom, which include the sanctity of the individual, have helped to shape our European societies. That is not to suggest that the church was always entirely faithful in practice, always and everywhere, to the insights of its gospel but, nevertheless, it remains true that a number of positive features of an evangelical heritage have become part of the shared patrimony of church and state in our time.

The term 'communion of saints' is a familiar and cherished notion within the Catholic culture and the communitarian dimension of the church which it implies. Catholic social teaching has always balanced the role of the individual in society with the claims of the wider community. Esteem for what is called the 'common good' and its welfare has always played an important part in the social application of gospel values. In its pastoral trends, illustrated especially by the movement of liberation theology in Latin and Central America, the Catholic Church has been community driven to the extent that it is often criticised by capitalist forces as being plain socialist in its bent, if not propounding even a Marxist dialectic. The truth is that the individual and the community are held in creative tension in orthodox Catholic social teaching.

The communion of saints connotes a relationship between Christians which is not confined to earthly existence but is rather marked by its dramatic inclusivity, extending to those who have already departed as well as those still living. For those who tend towards a maximalism in their theology of salvation, it is hard to know who, if any, are excluded from this spiritual family. Traditionally, the communion of saints evokes the memory of outstanding Christians who are honoured publicly by church authority, but in the Pauline understanding of the phrase it certainly includes at least all those baptised in Christ. It may be best described as that universal family of all God's graced sons and daughters, both those who have gone before us and those still on life's pilgrimage.

Looking on the Lough Derg pilgrimage population, Kavanagh focuses in one passage on the amorphous character of the crowd, largely undifferentiated as to personalities and personal histories. In this perspective he writes:

… the silver strands
Of the individual sometimes show
Through the fabric of prison anonymity.
One man's private trouble transcending the divinity
Of the prayer-locked multitude.

In these lines perhaps he is hinting that, despite the overwhelmingly corporate anatomy of the pilgrimage, there are important individual stories hidden away among the mass of pilgrims, waiting to be told. Again Kavanagh is alluding to the uniqueness of every individual person. He continues his theme of each person being individually present to 'God, the poet', who knows the recesses of the human heart and is, in the end, the only One who can 'write straight', so to speak, 'the crooked lines' of their lives' troubled course:

> The ex-monk, farmer and the girl
> Melted in the crowd
> Where only God, the poet
> Followed with interest till he found
> Their secret, and constructed from
> The chaos of its fire
> A reasonable document.

The timeless nature of the Christian event
> Was that St Paul
> Riding his ass down a lane in Donegal?
> Christ was lately dead,
> Men were afraid
> With a new fear, the fear
> Of love. There was a laugh freed
> For ever and for ever. The Apostles' Creed
> Was a fireside poem, the talk of the town ...
> They remember a man who has seen Christ in his thorny crown.

It has been noted earlier that each of the six headings representing the religious content of the poem are interconnected. Indeed, the above passage, with its evocation of both timelessness and contemporaneity regarding the Christian story, is closely linked with the theme of the communion of saints of the last section. Thus it symbolises the unique continuum of the Christian family across the centuries. It may be recalled that Kavanagh remarkably reported on his visit to Lough Derg in *The Standard* in 1942 that his 'first and strongest impression' was of the 'freshness and recency of Christianity', 'the excitement of the new truth ... stirring the imagination of men and women'. This particular and unusual impression is played out most engagingly in this passage of the poem. It has about it a strength and originality which are memorable. It might be said to bring to life in a unique way the biblical events of some two thousand years ago. The most crucial and prophetic lines may be that after the Christ event:

Men were afraid
With a new fear, the fear
Of love.

This suggests that the quality of love demonstrated by Jesus 'laying down his life for his friends' (cf. John 15:13) was of such a supreme order that those who followed were frightened by this example and the prospect of being expected to practise a love that was similarly selfless. After all, Jesus told his followers that they should love one another as he had loved them (cf. John 15:17). This level of loving is unsettling in its radicality. Someone has said, 'If you love well enough, you will be killed'! Something of an exciting, if sombre, truth lurks in that prediction. There is, moreover, a haunting and inspired irony in the poet's description of the Calvary event which he renders unexpectedly as 'a laugh, freed For ever and for ever'. This quintessential Kavanagh insight recalls his attachment to and celebration of what he called 'the comic vision' which has already been dealt with elsewhere in this study. Kavanagh's understanding of poetry, nurtured by the Comic Muse, and his interpretation of life's pilgrimage culminate for him in the conviction that the human person is ultimately saved by God. The final vindication of life's enterprise is to be found in the death and resurrection of the Lord. This is the source of the Christian's laughter, the laughter of unquenchable hope.

The puzzle of time, as experienced in the human condition, is something which must be landscaped into the macro-vision of the person of faith. Time is a condition of our lives here on earth. But in our consideration of transcendent realities we must somehow bracket the notion of time which is essentially a way of experiencing and measuring change. In our contemplation of the absolute we try to envisage a timeless universe and this we can only attempt by a bold stretch of the imagination. But some awareness of a state outside and beyond time is necessary as we confront the Christian mystery. In a homely way

Kavanagh's imaginative propinquity to historical figures, such as St Paul and Jesus himself – 'Yet he [Fitzsimons] alone went out with Jesus fishing' – brings them out of the restriction of time and into an artistically designed, continuous present.

Yet again in the poem Kavanagh introduces the idea of Jesus Christ 'yesterday, today and the same forever' (Hebrews 13:8). The character of Robert Fitzsimons, sceptical as he begins his pilgrimage on the island, is happy to talk academically about spiritual matters but shirks any form of personal involvement in the sacramental reality of worship and prayer:

> He skimmed the sentiment of every pool of experience
> And talked heresy lightly from distances
> Where nothing was terrifyingly Today
> Where he felt he could be safe and say or sin –
> But Christ sometimes bleeds in the museum.

Is there a reminder in this last line that Jesus Christ, his teaching and his life are not just historical events to be regarded as now well past and gone? For Kavanagh, Jesus is more and is believed by his community to be an ever-living presence in their midst. Christianity is not just a remarkable story, however wonderful and edifying. It is an experience through which we live today in his Body, the Christian Church. Christ suffered but also suffers in the present tense, as he still confronts evil in the world. We are in a current relationship with Christ as head of the Body of faith, hope and love to which we belong. Kavanagh makes the point, through the ruminations of Robert Fitzsimons. There can be no embalmed Christ or Christianity. He may not be relegated to a museum, however beautiful. He is the Lord of life and, as such, continues to dwell amongst us. The incarnation event guarantees a permanent 'now' for God's love at work in Christ among his people. Jesus is not, nor cannot be, superseded. Such a form of historicism evacuates Christianity of its trans-temporal relevance. The significance and immediacy of Christ to his people, so far from waning over time, actually grows and develops. The fuller meaning of a person or of an event becomes apparent only over time and within the context of our relationship in the here and now to that person and that event. This is a key understanding in our apprehension of the mystery of Christ and his resurrection, made present in the liturgy. Kavanagh's imagination is attempting, I believe, to express this reality.

Lough Derg

From Cavan and from Leitrim and from Mayo,
From all the thin-faced parishes where hills
Are perished noses running peaty water,
They come to Lough Derg to fast and pray and beg
With all the bitterness of nonentities, and the envy
Of the inarticulate when dealing with an artist.
Their hands push closed the doors that God holds open.
Love-sunlit is an enchanter in June's hours
And flowers and light. These to shopkeepers and small lawyers
Are heresies up beauty's sleeve.

The naïve and simple go on pilgrimage too,
Lovers trying to take God's truth for granted ...
Listen to the chanted
Evening devotions in the limestone church,
For this is Lough Derg, St Patrick's Purgatory.
He came to this island-acre of greenstone once
To be shut of the smug too-faithful. The story
Is different now.
Solicitors praying for cushy jobs
To be County Registrar or Coroner,
Shopkeepers threatened with sharper rivals
Than any hook-nosed foreigner.
Mothers whose daughters are Final Medicals,
Too heavy-hipped for thinking,
Wives whose husbands have angina pectoris,
Wives whose husbands have taken to drinking.

But there were the sincere as well,
The innocent who feared the hell
Of sin. The girl who had won
A lover and the girl who had none

Were both in trouble
Trying to encave in the rubble
Of these rocks the Real,
The part that can feel.
And the half-pilgrims too,
They who are the true
Spirit of Ireland, who joke
Through the Death-mask and take
Virgins of heaven or flesh,
Were on Lough Derg Island
Wanting some half-wish.

Over the black waves of the lake trip the last echoes
Of the bell that has shooed through the chapel door
The last pilgrims, like hens to roost.
The sun through Fermanagh's furze fingers
Looks now on the deserted penance rings of stone
Where only John Flood on St Kevin's Bed lingers
With the sexton's heaven-sure stance, the man who knows
The ins and outs of religion …
'Hail glorious St Patrick' a girl sings above
The old-man drone of the harmonium.
The rosary is said and Benediction.
The Sacramental sun turns round and 'Holy, Holy, Holy'
The pilgrims cry, striking their breasts in Purgatory.

The same routine and ritual now
As serves for street processions or Congresses
That take all shapes of souls as a living theme
In a novel refuses nothing. No truth oppresses.

Women and men in bare feet turn again
To the iron crosses and the rutted Beds,
Their feet are swollen and their bellies empty –

But something that is Ireland's secret leads
These petty mean people
For here's the day of a poor soul freed
To a marvellous beauty above its head.
The Castleblaney grocer trapped in the moment's need
Puts out a hand and writes what he cannot read,
A wisdom astonished at every turn
By some angel that writes in the oddest words.
When he will walk again in Muckno Street
He'll hear from the kitchens of fair-day eating houses
In the after-bargain carouses
News from a country beyond the range of birds.

The lake waves caught the concrete stilts of the Basilica
That spread like a bulldog's hind paws. A Leitrim man,
With a face as sad as a flooded hay-field,
Leaned in an angle of the walls with his rosary beads in his hands.

Beside St Brigid's Cross – an ancient relic
A fragment of the Middle Ages set
Into the modern masonry of the conventional Basilica
Where everything is ordered and correct –
A queue of pilgrims waiting to renounce
The World, the Flesh, the Devil and all his house.

Like young police recruits being measured
Each pilgrim flattened backwards to the wall
And stretched his arms wide
As he cried:
'I renounce the World, the Flesh and the Devil';
Three times they cried out. A country curate
Stared with a curate leer – he was proud.
The booted
Prior passes by ignoring all the crowd.

'I renounce the World,' a young woman cried.
Her breasts stood high in the pagan sun,
'I renounce …' an old monk followed. Then a fat lawyer.
They rejected one by one
The music of Time's choir.

A half-pilgrim looked up at the Carrara marbles,
St Patrick wearing an alb with no stitch dropped.
Once he held a shamrock in his hand
But the stem was flawed and it got lost.

St Brigid and the Blessed Virgin flanked
Ireland's national apostle
On the south-west of the island on the gravel-path
Opposite the men's hostel.

Around the island like soldiers quartered round a barrack-yard
There were houses, and a stall where agnisties
And Catholic Truth pamphlets were sold,
And at the pier end, the grey chapel of St Mary's.

The middle of the island looked like the memory
Of some village evicted by the Famine,
Some corner of a field beside a well
Old stumps of walls where a stunted boortree is growing.
These were the holy cells of saintly men –
O that was the place where Mickey Fehan lived
And the Reillys before they went to America in the Fifties.
No, this is Lough Derg in County Donegal –
So much alike is our historical
And spiritual pattern, a heap
Of stones anywhere is consecrated
By love's terrible need.

On Lough Derg, too, the silver strands
Of the individual sometimes show
Through the fabric of prison anonymity.
One man's private trouble transcending the divinity
Of the prayer-locked multitude.
A vein of humanity that can bleed
Through the thickest hide.
And such a plot unfolds a moment, so –

In a crevice between the houses and the lake
A tall red-headed man of thirty slouches,
A half-pilgrim who hated prayer,
All truth for which St Patrick's Purgatory vouches.
He was a small farmer who was fond of literature
In a country-schoolmaster way.
He skimmed the sentiment of every pool of experience
And talked heresy lightly from distances
Where nothing was terrifyingly Today
Where he felt he could be safe and say or sin –
But Christ sometimes bleeds in the museum.
It was the first day of his pilgrimage.
He came to Lough Derg to please the superstition
Which says, 'At least the thing can do no harm'
Yet he alone went out with Jesus fishing.

An ex-monk from Dublin, a broad-faced man
With his Franciscan habit sweeping was a pilgrim
A sad priest staggering in a megrim
Between doubt and vanity's courtesan.
He had fallen once and secretly, no shame
Tainted the young girl's name,
A convent schoolgirl knowing
Nothing of earth sowing.

He took her three times
As in his day-dreams
These things happened.
Three times finds all
The notes of body's madrigal.
'Twas a failing otherwise
Lost him his priestly faculties.

Barefoot in the kitchen
Of John Flood's cottage
Where the girls of Donegal sat, laughing round on stools,
And iron cranes and crooks
Were loaded with black pots,
And holy-looking women kept going in and out of the rooms
As though some man was a-waking …
The red-haired man came in
And saw among the loud cold women one who
Was not a Holy Biddy
With a rat-trap on her diddy,
But something from the unconverted kingdom
The beauty that has turned
Convention into forests
Where Adam wanders deranged with half a memory;
And red-haired Robert Fitzsimons
Saw Aggie Meegan, and quietly
An angel was turning over the pages of Mankind's history.
He must have her, she was waiting
By the unprotected gable
Of asceticism's granite castle. The masonry's down
And the sun coming in is blood
The green of trees is lust
He saw from the unpeopled country into a town.

Let beauty bag or burst,
The sharp points of truth may not be versed
Too smoothly, but the truth must go in as it occurred,
A bulb of light in the shadows of Lough Derg.

The first evening they prayed till nine o'clock
Around the gravel rings, a hundred decades
Of rosaries until they hardly knew what words meant –
Their own names when they spoke them sounded mysterious.
They knelt and prayed and rose and prayed
And circled the crosses and kissed the stones
Never looking away from the brimstone bitterness
To the little islands of Pan held in the crooked elbow of the lake.
They closed their eyes to Donegal and the white houses
On the slope of the northern hills.

And these pilgrims of a western reason
Were not pursuing French-hot miracles.
There were hundreds of them tripping one another
Upon the pilgrim way (O God of Truth,
Keep him who tells this story straight,
Let no cheap insincerity shape his mouth).
These men and boys were not led there
By priests of Maynooth or stories of Italy or Spain
For this is the penance of the poor
Who know what beauty hides in misery
As beggars, fools and eastern fakirs know.

Black tea, dry bread.
Yesterday's pilgrims went upstairs to bed
And as they slept
The vigil in St Patrick's prison was kept
By the others. The Evening Star

Looked into Purgatory whimsically. Night dreams are
Simple and catching as music-hall tunes
Of the Nineties. We'll ramble through the brambles of
    starry-strange Junes.

On a seat beside the women's hostel four men
Sat and talked spare minutes away;
It was like Sunday evening on a country road
Light and gay.
The talk was 'There's a man
Who must be twenty stone weight – a horrid size …'
'Larry O'Duff … yes, like a balloon
Or a new tick of chaff … Lord , did anyone ever see clearer skies?'
'No rain a while yet, Joe,
And the turnips could be doing with a sup, you know.'

And in the women's talk too, was woven
Such earth to cool the burning brain of Heaven.
On the steps of the church the monks talked
To Robert of art, music, literature.
'Genius is not measured,' he said,
'In prudent feet and inches
Old Justice burns the work of Raphael –
Justice was God until he saw His Son
Falling in love with earth's fantastic one,
The woman in whose dunghill of emotion
Grows flowers of poetry, music, and the old
Kink in the mind, the fascination
Of sin troubled the mind of God
Until He thought of Charity …
Have you known Charity? Have I?'
Aggie Meegan passed by
To vigil. Robert was puzzled, Where

Grew the germ of this crooked prayer?
The girl was thrilling as joy's despair.

A schoolmaster from Roscommon led
The vigil prayers that night.
'Hail Queen of Heaven' they sang at twelve.
Someone snored near the porch. A bright
Moon sailed in from the County Tyrone
By the water route that he might make
Queer faces in the stained-glassed windows. Why should sun
Have all the fun?
'Our vows of Baptism we again take …'
Every Rosary brought the morning nearer.
The schoolmaster looked at his watch and said:
'Out now for a mouthful of fresh air –
A ten-minute break to clear the head.'
It was cold in the rocky draughts between the houses.
Old women tried
To pull bare feet close to their bellies.
Three o'clock rang from the Prior's house clock.
In the hostels pilgrims slept away a three-day fast.

On the cell-wall beside the sycamore tree,
The tree that never knew a bird,
Aggie sat fiddling with her Rosary
And doubting the power of Lough Derg
To save the season's rose of life
With the ponderous fingers of prayer's philosophy.

Robert was a philosopher, a false one
Who ever takes a sledge to swat a fly.
He talked to the girls as a pedant professor
Talking in a university.

The delicate precise immediacy
That sees a flower half a foot away
He could not learn. He spoke to Aggie
Of powers, passions, with the *naïveté*
Of a ploughman. She did not understand –
She only knew that she could hold his hand
If he stood closer. 'Virtue is sublime,'
He said, 'and it is virtue is the frame
Of all love and learning ...'
'I want to tell you something,' she whispered,
'Because you are different and will know ...'
'You don't need to tell me anything, you could not,
For your innocence is pure glass that I see through.'
'You'd be surprised,' she smiled. O God, he gasped
To his soul, what could she mean by that?
They watched the lake waves clapping cold hands together
And saw the morning breaking as it breaks
Over a field where a man is watching a calving cow.
New life, new day.
A half-pilgrim saw it as a rabbiter
Poaching in wood sees
Primeval magic among the trees.

The rusty cross of St Patrick had a dozen
Devotees clustered around it at four o'clock.
Bare knees were going round St Brendan's Bed.
A boy was standing like a ballet dancer poised on the rock
Under the belfry; he stared over at Donegal
Where the white houses on the side of the hills
Popped up like mushrooms in September.
The sun was smiling on a thousand hayfields
That hour, and he must have thought Lough Derg
More unreasonable than ordinary stone.

Perhaps it was an iceberg
That he had glanced at on his journey from Japan,
But the iceberg filled a glass of water
And poured it to the honour of the sun.
Lough Derg in the dawn poured rarer cups. Prayer
And fast that makes the sourest drink rare.
Was that St Paul
Riding his ass down a lane in Donegal?
Christ was lately dead,
Men were afraid
With a new fear, the fear
Of love. There was a laugh freed
For ever and for ever. The Apostles' Creed
Was a fireside poem, the talk of the town ...
They remember a man who has seen Christ in his thorny crown.

John Flood came out and climbed the rock to ring
His bell for six o'clock. He spoke to the pilgrims:
'Was the night fine?'
'Wonderful, wonderful,' they answered, 'not too cold –
Thank God we have the worst part over us.'

The bell brought the sleepers from their cubicles.
Grey-faced boatmen were getting out a boat.
Mass was said. Another day began.
The penance wheel turned round again.
Pilgrims went out in boats, singing
'O Fare Thee Well, Lough Derg' as they waved
Affection to the persecuting stones.

The Prior went with them – suavely, goodily
Priestly, painfully directing the boats.

They who were left behind
Felt like the wellwishers who keep house when the funeral
Has left for the chapel.

Lough Derg overwhelmed the individual imagination
And the personal tragedy.
Only God thinks of the dying sparrow
In the middle of a war.

The ex-monk, farmer and the girl
Melted in the crowd
Where only God, the poet
Followed with interest till he found
Their secret, and constructed from
The chaos of its fire
A reasonable document.

A man's the centre of the world,
A man is not an anonymous
Member of the general public.
The Communion of Saints
Is a Communion of individuals.
God the Father is the Father
Of each one of us.

Then there was war, the slang, the contemporary touch,
The ideologies of the daily papers.
They must seem realer, Churchill, Stalin, Hitler,
Than ideas in the contemplative cloister.
The battles where ten thousand men die
Are more significant than a peasant's emotional problem.
But wars will be merely dry bones in histories
And these common people real living creatures in it

On the unwritten spaces between the lines.
A man throws himself prostrate
And God lies down beside him like a woman
Consoling the hysteria of her lover
That sighs his passion emptily:
'The next time, love, you shall faint in me.'

'Don't ask for life,' the monk said.
'If you meet her
Be easy with your affection;
She's a traitor
To those who love too much
As I have done.'
'What have you done?' said Robert
'That you've come
To St Patrick's Purgatory?'
The monk told his story
Of how he thought that he
Could make reality
Of the romance of the books
That told of Popes,
Men of genius who drew
Wild colours on the flat page. He knew
Now that madness is not knowing
That laws for the mown hay
Will not serve that which is growing.
Through Lough Derg's fast and meditation
He learned the wisdom of his generation.
He was satisfied now his heart
Was free from the coquetry of art.

Something was unknown
To Robert, not long,

For Aggie told him all
That hour as they sat on the wall
Of Brendan's cell:
Birth, bastardy and murder –
He only heard rocks crashing distantly
When John Flood rang the midday bell.

Now the three of them got out of the story altogether
Almost. Now they were not three egotists
But part of the flood of humanity,
Anonymous, never to write or be written.
They vanish among the forests and we see them
Appearing among the trees for seconds.
Lough Derg rolls its caravan before us
And as the pilgrims pass their thoughts are reckoned.
St Patrick was there, that peasant-faced man,
Whose image was embroidered on political banners
In the days of the AOH and John Redmond.
A kindly soft man this Patrick was, like a farmer
To whom no man might be afraid to tell a story
Of bawdy life as it goes in country places.
Was St Patrick like that?
A shamrock in a politician's hat
Yesterday. Today
The sentimentality of an Urban Councillor
Moving an address of welcome to the Cardinal.
All Ireland's Patricks were present on Lough Derg,
All Ireland that froze for want of Europe.

'And who are you?' said the poet speaking to
The old Leitrim man.
He said, 'I can tell you
What I am.

Servant girls bred my servility:
When I stoop
It is my mother's mother['s] mother's mother
Each one in turn being called in to spread –
"Wider with your legs," the master of the house said.
Domestic servants taken back and front.
That's why I'm servile. It is not the poverty
Of soil in Leitrim that makes me raise my hat
To fools with fifty pounds in a paper bank.
Domestic servants, no one has told
Their generations as it is, as I
Show the cowardice of the man whose mothers were whored
By five generations of capitalist and lord.'

Time passed.
Three boatloads of Dublin's unemployed came in
At three o'clock led by a priest from Thomas Street
To glutton over the peat-filtered water
And sit back drunk when jobs are found
In the Eternal factory where the boss
Himself must punch the clock.

And the day crawled lazily
Along the orbit of Purgatory.

A baker from Rathfriarland
A solicitor from Derry
A parish priest from Wicklow
A civil servant from Kerry
Sat on the patch of grass,
Their stations for the day
Completed – all things arranged,
Nothing in doubt, nothing gone astray.

O the boredom of Purgatory
Said the poet then,
This piety that hangs like a fool's, unthought,
This certainty in men,
This three days too-goodness,
Too-neighbourly cries
Temptation to murder
Mediocrities.

The confession boxes in St Mary's chapel hum
And it is evening now. Prose prayers become
Odes and sonnets.
There is a shrine with money heaped upon it
Before Our Lady of Miraculous Succour.

A woman said her litany:
That my husband may get his health
    We beseech thee hear us
That my son Joseph may pass the Intermediate
    We beseech thee hear us
That my daughter Eileen may do well at her music
    We beseech thee hear us
That her aunt may remember us in her will
    We beseech thee hear us
That there may be good weather for the hay
    We beseech thee hear us
That my indigestion may be cured
    We beseech thee hear us
O Mother of Perpetual Succour! in temptation
    Be you near us.
And some deep prayers were shaped like sonnets –

O good St Anthony, your poor client asks
That he may have one moment in his arms

The girl I am thinking of this minute –
I'd love her even if she had no farms
Or a four-footed beast in a stable;
Her father is old, doting down the lanes,
There isn't anyone as able
As I am for cocking hay or cleaning drains.
All this that I am is an engine running
Light down the narrow-gauge railway of life.
St Anthony, I ask for Mary Gunning
Of Rathdrumskean to be my wife.
My strength is a skull battering the wall
Where a remand-prisoner is losing his soul.

St Anne, I am a young girl from Castleblaney,
One of a farmer's six grown daughters.
Our little farm, when the season's rainy,
Is putty spread on stones. The surface waters
Soak all the fields of this north-looking townland.
Last year we lost our acre of potatoes
And my mother with unmarried daughters round her
Is soaked like our soil in savage natures.
She tries to be as kind as any mother
But what can a mother be in such a house
With arguments going on and such a bother
About the half-boiled pots and unmilked cows.
O Patron of the pure woman who lacks a man,
Let me be free I beg of you, St Anne.

O Sacred Heart of Jesus, I ask of you
A job so I can settle down and marry;
I want to live a decent life. And through
The flames of St Patrick's Purgatory
I go offering every stone-bruise, all my hunger;

In the back-room of my penance I am weaving
An inside-shirt for charity. How longer
Must a fifty-shilling-a-week job be day-dreaming?
The dole and empty minds and empty pockets,
Cup Finals seen from the branches of a tree,
Old films that break the eye-balls in their sockets,
A toss-pit. This is life for such as me.
And I know a girl and I know a room to be let
And a job in a builder's yard to be given yet.

I have sinned old; my lust's a running sore
That drains away my strength. Each morning shout:
'Last night will be the last! At fifty-four
A broken will's a bone that will not knit.
I slip on the loose rubble of remorse
And grasp at tufts of cocksfoot grass that yield,
My belly is a bankrupt's purse.

My mind is a thrice-failed cropping field
Where the missed ridges give out their ecstasy
To weeds that seed through gaps of indiscretion.
Nettles where barley or potatoes should be.
I set my will in Communion and Confession
But still the sore is dribbling – blood, and will
In spite of penance, prayer and canticle.

This was the banal
Beggary that God heard. Was he bored
As men are with the poor? Christ Lord
Hears in the voices of the meanly poor
Homeric utterances, poetry sweeping through.

More pilgrims came that evening
From the pier.
The old ones watched the boats come
And smothered the ridiculous cheer
That breaks, like a hole in pants,
Where the heroic armies advance.

Somebody bought a newspaper
With news of war.
When they lived in Time they knew
What men killed each other for –
Was it something different in the spelling
Of a useless law?

A man under the campanile said:
'Kipper is fish – nice.'
Somebody else talked of Dempsey:
'Greater than Tunney.' Then a girl's voice
Called: 'You'll get cigarettes inside.'

It was six o'clock in the evening.
Robert sat looking over the lake
Seeing the green islands that were his morning hope
And his evening despair.
The sharp knife of Jansen
Cuts all the green branches,
Not sunlight comes in
But the hot-iron sin
Branding the shame
Of a beast in the Name
Of Christ on the breast
Of a child of the West.
It was this he had read.

All day he was smitten
By this foul legend written
In the fields, in the skies,
In the sanctuaries.
But now the green tree
Of humanity
Was leafing again
Forgiveness of sin.
A shading hand over
The brow of the lover.

And as the hours of Lough Derg's time
Stretch long enough to hold a generation
He sat beside her and promised that no word
Of what he knew should ever be heard.
The bell at nine o'clock closed the last station,
The pilgrims kissed goodbye to stone and clay.
The Prior had declared the end of day.

Morning from the hostel windows was like the morning
In some village street after a dance carouse,
Debauchees of Venus and Bacchus
Half-alive stumbling wearily out of a bleary house.
So these pilgrims stumbled below in the sun
Out of God's public-house.

The Mass was said.
Pilgrims smiled at one another
How good God was
How much a loving Father!
How wonderful the punishing stones were!
Another hour and the boats will sail
Into the port of Time.
Are you not glad you came?

John Flood stared at the sky
And shook his proud head knowingly.
No storm, nor rain.
The boats are ready to sail.

The monk appears once more
Not trailing his robes as before
But different, his pride gone,
Green hope growing where the feet of Pan
Had hoofed the grass.
Lough Derg, St Patrick's Purgatory in Donegal,
Christendom's purge. Heretical
Around the edges: the centre's hard
As the commonsense of a flamboyant bard.
The twentieth century blows across it now
But deeply it has kept an ancient vow.
It knows the secret of pain –
O moralist, your preaching is in vain
To tell men of the germ in the grain.

All happened on Lough Derg as it is written
In June nineteen forty-two
When the Germans were fighting outside Rostov.
The poet wrote it down as best he knew
As integral and completed as the emotion
Of men and women cloaking a burning emotion
In the rags of the commonplace, will permit him.
He too was one of them. He too denied
The half of him that was his pride
Yet found it waiting, and the half untrue
Of this story is his pride's rhythm.

The turnips were a-sowing in the fields around Pettigo
As our train passed through.
A horse-cart stopped near the eye of the railway bridge.
By Monaghan and Cavan and Dundalk
By Bundoran and by Omagh the pilgrims went
And three sad people had found the key to the lock
Of God's delight in disillusionment.

Father Mat: Introduction

The parish priest has long been a singular and central figure in rural Ireland. His professional *persona* is well-known: traditionally, he has been represented as an authoritative and, more often than not, authoritarian presence in the community involved, through a variety of activities, in the formal Christian life of his locality. Strictly speaking, the priest's role is to preach the gospel and celebrate the sacraments among believers in the parish to which he is assigned. However, these essential functions are exercised by extension in any number of ministries which naturally flow out from them. Thus his ministry of the word of God will include, in addition to preaching in church, the promotion of a knowledge of Christian teaching among those in his parish. Normally the priest will be responsible for the religious instruction of children in school as he helps to prepare pupils for the sacraments in collaboration with teachers. In addition, he may help to organise various forms of adult Christian education and encourage a range of cultural projects which contribute to the human development of those in the neighbourhood. As a development of his eucharistic ministry, the priest will necessarily be engaged in local community-building, in whatever ways this is possible, since the growth of creative neighbourliness is implicit in the gathering of parishioners around the altar that is the Lord's table. In this context too, the priest is expected to be practically concerned for those who are deprived in the parish, attempting to fulfil the classical evangelical model of the pastor. The needs of the people at every level of their lives ought to be the object of his special interest and attention. The demands of the sick and the elderly will engage his sympathetic support as he visits them in their homes, in hospitals and other institutions. Besides, the priest is expected to make time for regular, prayerful reflection.

How the parish priest accomplishes his multiple pastoral tasks will depend on his capabilities and opportunities, which vary from priest to priest and from one parish to another. Nowadays, the parish priest attempts to fulfil his pastorate by organising groups of lay persons in the parish who will advise and assist across a wide spectrum of church responsibilities, which ultimately devolve on all the baptised members of the local Christian community. In recent times there has developed the practice of widespread delegation of pastoral services, such as the ministry of the Word and of the Eucharist, liturgical planning, preparation for baptism, bereavement counselling and home visitation. This latter day tradition has grown in response, mainly, to the insights of the Second Vatican Council (1962-5), which sees the priest as the facilitator of the corporate efforts of parishioners in promoting the gospel, rather than as a solo agent in the organisation and growth of the parish.

The priestly ministry has, of course, been designed and has worked historically, corresponding to various models of church in different eras.

An older model of church and parish, which obtained during Patrick Kavanagh's life growing up in Inniskeen, saw the priest as the person exclusively charged with the spiritual affairs of the community. For that reason his presence was experienced as somewhat larger than life. He was seen by parishioners as simply 'the church' in their midst, functioning in a monopolistic capacity. In times when ordinary people's horizons were largely confined to their own parish, their perceptions of what the Catholic Church represented were dictated by the style and performance of their local priest. In this respect it might be said that Catholic life reflected what in civic life was once famously described by the Irish American politician Tip O'Neill, when he declared 'all politics is local'. All church life too was local, although linked, subliminally at least, with a wider and larger reality.

In the Irish countryside the pastor was frequently what might be called a 'farmer-priest' in that a modest piece of land went with the often draughty and sometimes dilapidated residence known as the parochial house. As a consequence, the parish priest would keep some cattle and perhaps a horse or two in his fields. He would more often than not himself be of farming stock, so that his agricultural activity, such as it might be, bound him in a congenial way to his farming neighbours. This was so in the case of Kavanagh's parish priest, Fr

Bernard Maguire, who may be, although in a loose fashion, the model for the Father Mat of the poem.

The farmer-priest has become an extinct species in our time which indeed can now be said of all the stock clerical figures of Kavanagh's day. The Irish rural parish priest is found in stereotype in Irish literature, especially in the medium of drama. Living alone, though often cared for adjunctively by a housekeeper, he has more often than not been depicted as a solitary and perhaps eccentric figure, scholarly or otherwise, forbidding in manner, whose word was law. The parish priest of story and theatre is often and irresistibly endowed with the title 'canon', an ecclesiastical honorific which to some contemporary ears at least smacks of the quaint and the effete. Although Irish writers have been tempted to caricature the figure of the country parish priest, yet there are examples of fictional clerics which emerge in the literature as sensitive and saintly. In the case of Patrick Kavanagh, his priests, both in his prose and in the poem *Father Mat*, are sympathetic characters.

The poem *Father Mat* has been quarried by Kavanagh from a considerably longer and earlier poem entitled *Why Sorrow?* With the exception of just three stanzas, *Father Mat* is contained in its entirety in the former. The Father Mat of *Why Sorrow?* is a different figure to that in the poem that was later to bear his name as title. The priest in the earlier poem is a troubled figure whose character is gently resolved as he evolves in the subsequent work. The cleric in *Why Sorrow?* is frustrated by unfulfilled poetic aspirations and, though outwardly at ease in his community, is deep down unsettled in mind and heart. This may well represent Kavanagh's own self-doubts and conflictual mental state in the 1930s as he struggles to decide whether he should leave the confinement of his small, rural world of Inniskeen or remain to honour his familial obligations on the home place.

The autobiographical content of Kavanagh's *Why Sorrow?* may be detected in the quandary of the poet-priest character in that poem. Tempted to a loss of religious faith, he is oppressed by guilt as he senses the dependence on him manifested by his parishioners. His priestly ministry he regards as false, as he becomes enamoured of the pagan worldviews of the ancient Greek and Roman writers. The priest cogitates on his ambiguous situation as he is pulled towards another life of aesthetic enterprise. But the pastoral concern which binds him to his people cannot be discarded.

The priest's vocational paralysis mirrors Kavanagh's own efforts to move on to a new, more adventurous existence and a new brand of poetry. In *Why Sorrow?* Kavanagh is himself battling with the question of identity through the medium of Father Mat's indecision, but his attempt to clarify his own and Father Mat's dilemma in the poem remains, to his mind, unsuccessful. In the event, he switched to writing *The Great Hunger* and abandoned the priest-poet's spiritual odyssey of this long poem which remained unfinished. In real life, Kavanagh does in fact eventually make the break with his rural environment and leaves for his new urban life and all that it seemed to promise. The destiny of his *alter ego*, the priest, remains undecided at the end of the poem, but it is already apparent that he cannot abandon his priestly duties and the life to which he has solemnly committed himself.

The transformation in the Father Mat 1 of *Why Sorrow?* to the Father Mat 2 in the latter eponymous poem represents a major refinement, although vestiges of the first *persona* carry over into the second poem. This evolution seems to represent Kavanagh's own development from a state of religious turbulence and intellectual confusion in the 1930s to, in the 1940s, a new sense of literary direction and of spiritual resolution, together with the serenity that accrued therefrom. The particular fruits of Father Mat's progress from one poem to the other are the gentle, affectionate and affirmative lines that mark the character of the second poem, which came to bear the priest's name, in contrast to the sustained problematic of the earlier effort with its deliberately interrogative title *Why Sorrow?* In the substantially altered final version of the poem, Kavanagh distils a delicately fashioned, endearing figure from the labyrinthine excursions of its literary predecessor.

Father Mat: the poem

There is a healing quietude to the tone of this poem which offers a series of rich, lively images of the life of a rural parish. In the usual Kavanagh fashion the poet presents a cinematic montage of figures and events of normal living in his local neighbourhood, combined with reflective commentary on the symbolic universe that attends the rhythms of the parish religious calendar. It is the first Saturday of May. It was customary to hold evening devotions each day during this month, which would be reasonably well attended. The devotions consisted of the recitation of the rosary, followed by a sermon, as it was then called, and concluding with benediction. This liturgy would include public prayer, congregational singing of hymns, the offering of incense in the presence of the reserved sacrament in the monstrance before the blessing. Afterwards, there was a special opportunity for a chat among neighbours as they dispersed from the church. The central figure of the poem is the parish priest, Father Mat, who heard the monthly confessions after benediction on the first Saturday of each month. The attendance would be augmented on this occasion, as men as well as women arrived to go to Confession in preparation for Holy Communion at Mass on the Sunday morning following.

It is interesting that Kavanagh choses the May devotions as the setting for this poem. The month of May is traditionally associated with Mary, the Mother of God, who the poet here describes as 'the Queen of the May, the Virgin Mary with the schoolgirl air'. Kavanagh professed his warm faith in the Virgin Mary in his autobiographical work, *The Green Fool*. Two poems in honour of Mary are included in this anthology, *The Lady of the Poets* and *Our Lady's Tumbler*.

The poem moves between outdoor vignettes of farming folk and their animals and fowl as they engage in various rural routines, and indoor moments in the church itself. Father Mat's leisurely arrival at the church is described, as is his sacramental activity within it and his ruminative return to his parochial residence at the conclusion of the church gathering. During the course of the poem two humorous incidents are observed to occur, adding piquancy to the narrative: the old priest's young assistant or curate is briefly sighted by his senior, only to be mentally dismissed as an ambitious ecclesiocrat bent on organisation and efficiency and altogether without aptitude to appreciate the spell-binding mysterious beauty of nature. The second humorous insight, though conjectural, plots the innocent collision of prayerful intentions between a hopeful young man and a fervent young woman, each petitioning the intercession of Mary the Mother of God on their personal behalf. But, arguably, the most memorable passage of the poem is the manifestation of Father Mat's pastoral gentleness as he absolves in Christ's name the penitents who visit him in the confessional. Noteworthy in the poem is the priest's interior dialogue which alludes to three distinct gospel passages: the Holy Spirit's ubiquitous presence in the lives of all (cf John 3:8), the Sermon on the Mount (cf Matthew 5:3) and the Temptations of Christ (cf Matthew 4:1-11 and Luke 4:1-13).

The atmospheric details of the poem suggest topics, instinct in Kavanagh's verse, which may be examined under two headings: Ritual and Tradition and Nature and Grace.

Ritual and Tradition

In *The Green Fool*, Patrick Kavanagh lavishly declared: 'St Patrick loved the druids for their poetry and learning and incorporated in his Christianity the rich colours and the mystical depths of the older faith.'

The story of earliest Christianity in Ireland is remarkable in several respects. The Patrician flowering of the new faith seems to have taken place, in a sense, unobtrusively – a low-key drama enacted neither violently nor portentously. Unlike other countries, there were no martyrs in the Irish Christian dawn. The new dispensation arrived without bloodshed. The Patrician genius seems to have been the ability to graft the story of Christ and Mary and the saints on to the pre-existing religious culture. The ancient rituals surrounding it, related to mountains, wells and woods were, as it is said, 'baptised' and thus integrated into the new religious order. Saints were substituted for gods and goddesses. The god Lugh, from which *Lughnasa* (August) gets its name, was replaced by Patrick with the same, now intercessory, powers to protect crops, to lend importance to a certain place, and to overcome the forces of evil. Irish saints were heroic figures like those of early mythologies. Sacred gatherings became pilgrimages, and one did the rounds of a stone or hill or well. The gatherings in each place developed a link with a particular saint and became known as 'patterns', from the word 'patron'. Moreover, the four great festivals of the old Irish Celtic year, occurring in the middle of the four solar solstices, were newly appropriated. *Samhain* (1 November) became the feast of All Souls commemorating the dead. *Imbolg* (1 February), at the start of tilling, went to St Brigid with a plethora of rituals involving masks and Biddy Boys, some of which have continued down to our own time. *Bealtaine* (1 May) of the goddess caring for the cattle returning to pasture, transferred to Mary the Mother of God. *Lughnasa* (1 August), because of the roistering associated with the festival was not tolerated for long and failed to become permanently incorporated in the Christian calendar. Yet it survived in attenuated form in Irish folk religion as Garland Sunday, an occasion still remembered in the Irish countryside. It is clear that the Catholicism of the people in rural Ireland inherited an exceptionally rich repository of religious folk rituals from time immemorial.

In the middle of the nineteenth century, however, a reform of Irish Catholic practice, spearheaded by Cardinal Paul Cullen and abetted by the social weakening resulting from the Great Famine, did much to obliterate the old rituals and religious customs which had so fascinatingly blended pre-Christian and Christian symbols and rites in everyday Irish religious life. The old culture was displaced without any effort at re-adaptation in a form acceptable to orthodox practices. Again in the immediate aftermath of the Famine, sexual behaviour, sin and death were increasingly linked in the minds of the people. All too obviously, there had been too many mouths to feed in the 1840s and so high fertility and all that went with it for men and women was discouraged, leading to a cultural tension with regard to sexual activity and, in turn, to a new emphasis on the sacrament of Confession. It is this latter ritual which is featured in the poem *Father Mat*. Traces of land-based ritual, the oldest of all for mankind, make their way into the poem. Father Mat's preoccupation with fields, grass, ditches and earth in the context of his sacramental function as a confessor, retrieves remnants of the oldest of Irish symbolism. In the poem, which opens significantly with the phrase 'In a meadow', we read:

> ... the old priest is thinking
> His field of fresh grass, his horses, his cows,
> His earth into the fires of Purgatory.
> It cools his mind.
> 'They confess to the fields,' he mused,
> 'They confess to the fields and the air and the sky,'
> And forgiveness was the soft grass of his meadow by the river;
> His thoughts were walking through it now.

Hints of land-based ritual are not confined to this particular priest in his sacramental *persona*. In the current eucharistic liturgy we find this motif peeping into worship in the offertory prayers of the Mass, which come from the ancient Berakah prayers of Judaism which, in turn, reflect even older land-based rituals.

> Blessed are you, Lord God of all creation. Through your goodness
> we have this bread to offer which earth has given ...

At another point in the poem *Father Mat* is, stopping to

> Stare through gaps at ancient Ireland sweeping
> In again with all its unbaptised beauty ...

Kavanagh is aware of the primacy of creation and the mystery and the blessedness of the earth as a religious well-spring of the Irish people. In recent years, indeed since Kavanagh's death in 1967, there has been a renewed appreciation in Catholic theology of the sacredness of Planet Earth and the need to protect, savour and celebrate the gift of our environment.

The beauty of nature is God's first gift to us in his creation. As such, it is always 'baptised' in the sense that it is a symbol of God's generous providence in which we share, whether it be the 'good earth' or streams or rivers, symbols of continuous life and refreshment, or woods and forests which delight us with their grandeur, shades and smells.

Running through Kavanagh's nature-centred thought in *Father Mat* is a conviction that is echoed in no less a text than the Catholic Eucharistic Prayer at Mass, which reminds us that 'All creation rightly gives you [God] praise. All life, all holiness comes from you ....' It is artificial and indeed wrong to make sharp divisions or a dichotomy between created goodness and beauty and institutionally circumscribed objects of veneration and devotion. This dualism, which Kavanagh abhorred, rings untrue to our profession of faith in the Christian God in his ever-creative energy and presence, so forcefully expressed in the old Irish word *neart*, which expressly covers this understanding of the Godhead. By the same token, the ordinary activities of living were also seen by our Catholic ancestors as intimately related to God's own life, whose immanent presence in all our labours and leisure was celebrated in the detailed prayers for all occasions, so cherished in Irish traditional religion. These were the *Paidreacha Dúchais* or folk prayers: prayers for rising, for going to bed, for milking the cows, for raking the fire, for seeing the moon. These special prayer-rituals were used as a technique for building up an awareness of God to whom one was united at every hand's turn.

The naturalness with which the Irish people acknowledged God's presence is symbolised in the poem *Father Mat* in the obvious intimacy of the priest's presence among his people. His existence among them is connatural with their own. There is nothing extrinsic about God in our world, no less than about Father Mat around and about the parish:

He was a part of the place,
Natural as a round stone in a grass field;
He could walk through a cattle fair
And the people would only notice his odd spirit there.

The pronounced affinity between Father Mat, as a symbol of grace, with his natural habitat, the parish, may be seen as an analogue which illuminates the larger religious question of how nature and grace are interwoven in our world.

Nature and Grace

> Through the open door the hum of rosaries
> Came out and blended with the homing bees.
> > The trees
> Heard nothing stranger than the rain or the wind
> Or the birds –
> But deep in their roots they knew a seed had sinned.

In this passage Kavanagh identifies an unlikely communality between parishioners at prayer and their insect neighbours, joined by a similarity of pleasing sound. Both are part of God's creation. This may be read also as a wedding of grace and nature: grace sought through formal prayer corresponding to the bees in the fulfilment of their natural God-given function.

There was a time when the domain of grace was thought to be accessed only through religious and devotional activity. Ordinary life occupations, not designated as 'holy', were somehow of lesser merit than explicit worship of God in church. The reality is, however, that nature and grace are not easy to define independently of each other. Not so long ago, theological enquiry concerning the distinction between nature and grace proposed a strait-jacketed model. Each was presented as belonging to a different order of reality. This was so because the 'natural' and 'supernatural' were differentiated so that, for example, an animal (or a bee!) enjoyed a 'natural' existence while a human being was endowed with an additional and exclusive 'supernatural' dimension to his or her life.

The supernatural domain was that inhabited by divine life, i.e. grace, which survived, waxed or waned, depending largely on levels of moral performance.

This scheme bred its own form of dualism within the Christian life.

Natural and supernatural virtue were not to be confused. This categorical division did not, of course, in practice prevent men and women from reaching a state of genuine holiness, but such a spiritual dichotomy was unsatisfactory in a Christian culture which increasingly thought, worked, lived and prayed in what is now called a holistic manner. St Thomas Aquinas had declared, it is true, that 'grace builds on nature' but the contemporary theological mind-set would stretch this dictum further still, so that one apprehends the spiritual development of a Christian as an integrated phenomenon. The natural and graced elements of the personality mesh in a unitary dynamic, combining to form a model which is seen as a continuum of Christian growth rather than that of twin compartments catering for distinctly separate orders of being. Dismantling an excessive dualism in this respect does not mean the abolition of God's radically enabling support for one's spiritual aspirations and endeavours. Thus, as a *sine qua non* of the Christian quest, the free gift we call grace is never absent from our efforts. Nor does the unified understanding of nature and grace imply a Pelagian style reductionism which contests the primacy of grace in the Christian economy. 'We know that by turning everything to their good, God co-operates with all those who love him, with all those he has called according to his purpose.' (Rom 8:28)[31]

Kavanagh's embracing of the human person within wider nature would lay no claim to theological exactitude, which the poet never does. Nevertheless, he points up in his own way the essential unity of nature throughout all its realms and thus affirms the primacy of God's creation.

The last lines in the passage quoted above hint at a further truth of creation. These may, in the first instance, symbolise the silent witness of nature itself (the trees) to the failings and transgressions of parishioners confessing in church. In a wider sweep of the religious imagination, is the poet implying ('But deep in their roots they knew a seed had sinned') that God's saving love must always confront the mystery of evil? Despite the fundamental relationship of origin and inter-dependence between Creator, creature and creation, nevertheless some primal disorder persists *au fond* on our planet and in the human condition, by which both remain ineluctably estranged from each other and from God.

A consideration of nature as it relates to grace leads to the two major mysteries of the Christian faith and tradition: creation and incarnation. Among the early fathers of the church we find an acknowledgement of the universal presence of God in the world as a 'first grace' which is completed by the 'second grace' of Christ's coming. These first and second gifts are deduced from a complementary unity between creation and incarnation. Based on the doctrine of creation, mankind can be said to be graced from the beginning, in accordance with the revelation of the universal saving will of God in Christ (1 Timothy 4:10). In our time, theologian Karl Rahner emphasised that 'the grace of God has always been there ahead of our preaching'. The Christian message is not to be construed as 'something alien from outside but the awakening of something within, as yet not understood but nevertheless really present'. This view sees the Christ event as exercising, as it were, a retrospective function. This fits well into a spiritual landscape which enfolds both nature and grace. In this perspective grace, the gift of God's love to us, becomes an indivisible endowment.

The nature and grace question also arises in another historical context in the Father Mat of the earlier poem *Why Sorrow?*, already dealt with by way of background. The priest in that poem is torn between his attachment to the pre-Christian Greek and Roman deities and the Christian revelation in which he finds himself enclosed as he sees it. He even tries to reconcile the two as he speaks of 'Apollo's writing in a Christian hand'. The Roman goddess Venus, competes with the 'domestic Virgin and her Child' in Mat's imagination. It is interesting to recall that the great pre-Christian thinkers of antiquity (whatever about the gods and godesses) enjoyed a quasireligious esteem in the minds of some late medieval Catholic scholars. The ancient Greeks and Romans, in many instances, foreshadowed the teachings of Christianity, as the ambivalent Father Mat of *Why Sorrow?* speculates in a line from that poem, 'But the gospel was printed over an older writing'. Cicero pointed towards the radical altruism of the New Testament when he wrote in his *De Officis:* 'we are not born for ourselves alone' (*non nobis solum nati sumus*). Interestingly, St Paul, addressing the Athenians, insisted to them that 'the God whom I proclaim is in fact the one you already worship without knowing it'. He went on to quote approvingly for them from their own philosopher Epimenides, who had earlier suggested that God is not far from any of us 'Since it is in him that we live and move and have our being' (Acts: 17:28). In particular, the sixteenth-century Catholic priest and humanist, Erasmus of Rotterdam, was famous in his regard for the spiritual philosophy of the pre-Christian Greek and Roman writings, which converged in many respects with what he called 'the philosophy of Christ'. In his work *The Godly Feast*, he even offers the invocation 'Saint Socrates, pray for us' (to the outrage, let it be said, of his contemporary, Martin Luther!) Nevertheless, Erasmus was clear on the unique character of the Bible and, although eirenic in his inter-cultural outlook, he eschewed all forms of religious synchretism. In the light of all this, we can see why Father Mat, in his *Why Sorrow? persona,* was captivated by classical culture, faint traces of which cross over into the final *Father Mat* poem which we have been considering.

Father Mat

I

In a meadow
Beside the chapel three boys were playing football.
At the forge door an old man was leaning
Viewing a hunter-hoe. A man could hear
If he listened to the breeze the fall of wings –
How wistfully the sin-birds come home!

It was Confession Saturday, the first
Saturday in May; the May Devotions
Were spread like leaves to quieten
The excited armies of conscience.
The knife of penance fell so like a blade
Of grass that no one was afraid.

Father Mat came slowly walking, stopping to
Stare through gaps at ancient Ireland sweeping
In again with all its unbaptized beauty:
The calm evening,
The whitethorn blossoms,
The smell from ditches that were not Christian.
The dancer that dances in the hearts of men cried:
Look! I have shown this to you before –
The rags of living surprised
The joy in things you cannot forget.

His heavy hat was square upon his head,
Like a Christian Brother's;
His eyes were an old man's watery eyes,
Out of his flat nose grew spiky hairs.
He was a part of the place,

Natural as a round stone in a grass field;
He could walk through a cattle fair
And the people would only notice his odd spirit there.

His curate passed on a bicycle –
He had the haughty intellectual look
Of the man who never reads in brook or book;
A man designed
To wear a mitre,
To sit on committees –
For will grows strongest in the emptiest mind.

The old priest saw him pass
And, seeing, saw
Himself a medieval ghost.
Ahead of him went Power,
One who was not afraid when the sun opened a flower,
Who was never astonished
At a stick carried down a stream
Or at the undying difference in the corner of a field.

      II
The Holy Ghost descends
At random like the muse
On wise man and fool,
And why should poet in the twilight choose?

Within the dim chapel was the grey
Mumble of prayer
To the Queen of May –
The Virgin Mary with the schoolgirl air.

Two guttering candles on a brass shrine
Raised upon the wall
Monsters of despair
To terrify deep into the soul.

Through the open door the hum of rosaries
Came out and blended with the homing bees.
                    The trees
Heard nothing stranger than the rain or the wind
Or the birds –
But deep in their roots they knew a seed had sinned.

In the graveyard a goat was nibbling at a yew,
The cobbler's chickens with anxious looks
Were straggling home through nettles, over graves.
A young girl down a hill was driving cows
To a corner at the gable-end of a roofless house.

Cows were milked earlier,
The supper hurried,
Hens shut in,
Horses unyoked,
And three men shaving before the same mirror.

                    III
The trip of iron tips on tile
Hesitated up the middle aisle,
Heads that were bowed glanced up to see
Who could this last arrival be.

Murmur of women's voices from the porch,
Memories of relations in the graveyard.
On the stem
Of memory imaginations blossom.

                    In the dim
Corners in the side seats faces gather,
Lit up now and then by a guttering candle
And the ghost of day at the window.
A secret lover is saying
Three Hail Marys that she who knows
The ways of women will bring
Cathleen O'Hara (he names her) home to him.
Ironic fate! Cathleen herself is saying
Three Hail Marys to her who knows
The ways of men to bring
Somebody else home to her –
'O may he love me.'
What is the Virgin Mary now to do?

          IV
            From a confessional
The voice of Father Mat's absolving
Rises and falls like a briar in the breeze.
As the sins pour in the old priest is thinking
His fields of fresh grass, his horses, his cows,
His earth into the fires of Purgatory.
It cools his mind.
'They confess to the fields,' he mused,
'They confess to the fields and the air and the sky,'
And forgiveness was the soft grass of his meadow by the river;
His thoughts were walking through it now.

His human lips talked on:
'My son,
Only the poor in spirit shall wear the crown;
Those down
Can creep in the low door
On to Heaven's floor.'

The Tempter had another answer ready:
'Ah lad, upon the road of life
'Tis best to dance with Chance's wife
And let the rains that come in time
Erase the footprints of the crime.'

The dancer that dances in the hearts of men
Tempted him again:
'Look! I have shown you this before;
From this mountain-top I have tempted Christ
With what you see now
Of beauty – all that's music, poetry, art
In things you can touch every day.

I broke away
And rule all dominions that are rare;
I took with me all the answers to every prayer
That young men and girls pray for: love, happiness, riches –
O Tempter! O Tempter!

                    V
As Father Mat walked home
Venus was in the western sky
And there were voices in the hedges:
'God the Gay is not the Wise.'

'Take your choice, take your choice,'
Called the breeze through the bridge's eye.
'The domestic Virgin and Her Child
Or Venus with her ecstasy.'

Epilogue

Religious, poetic, and perhaps all language, is metaphorical. Metaphor, properly understood, is the medium of such basic religious statements as 'God came down from heaven' or 'Jesus is the Son of God'. They are the means by which we try to say that life is not exhausted by its physical and material limitations. Many biblical stories are extended metaphors, through which realities that transcend the literal are expressed. To take these stories in other terms, to say that they are either historical or false, is a reductionist approach which misses the meaning and transformative significance that the stories have had in contexts far removed from those that gave rise to them. These stories have established themselves as classic expressions of faith, not because they report historical events but because they have responded to the hopes and fears of countless generations, by giving a verbal form to fundamental convictions relating to what is ultimately true.

Where religious language is concerned, St Thomas Aquinas in his *Summa Theologica* makes the elementary, but important, observation: *'fides non terminatur in verbo sed in re'*, which, loosely translated, means faith does not stop at the word, is not fulfilled in words but rather in the reality beyond the words.

The Catholic tradition, for all its cultural outcroppings, is concerned essentially with a religious faith which is born out of story, that of Jesus Christ. The word for story in Greek is *muthos*, from which comes the term 'myth'. The Catholic religious enterprise accommodates both faith commitment *and* myth. Myth is a story that enters the imagination in such a way as to provide it with continuous nourishment. Myth is too often popularly regarded as a genre of unacceptable naïvete and nothing more than make-believe. This is not so. Myth is the vehicle by which symbolic reality, both simple and complex, is communicated to us in every era. This is true whether it applies to sporting icons, political figures or our understanding of human origins, purpose and transcendence. It can be an agent of disclosure for elemental and powerful truths. It invites us continuously to discover and forge fresh and rewarding religious insights. The key to understanding the nature of myth is to remember that myth is itself actually a particular kind of metaphor. As in ordinary discourse, we relegate dead and out-dated metaphors, so also unfruitful myths are likewise discarded. For that reason one does not ask whether a given myth is 'true or false' but, rather, whether it is 'living or dead'.

For Kavanagh, the believer, the mythology of Catholicism provided a mainstay for his poetic vision. He engaged in his own personal dialectic with his tradition and, in the process, repossessed for us in a fresh manner perennial Christian images and insights. This achievement may become apparent from a reading and re-reading of the poems in this collection.

The poet resembles the prophet in that he sees the same things as others but in a different way. He is aware of the Being that is present and manifest in particular beings, with all the excitement and satisfaction that this engenders. Kavanagh, in many ways, accomplishes this task and by so doing enriches our Catholic imagination. The Inniskeen man is both celebrant and seer within his own religious tradition.

Notes

Notes to Introduction
Poems marked with an asterisk in the introduction are not included in full in this anthology.

1. William Butler Yeats, originally from Sligo, was awarded the Nobel Prize for Literature in 1923. Seamus Heaney, a Derry man, became a Nobel Laureate in 1995.

2. P. Kavanagh, *Collected Pruse*. All subsequent prose quotations from Kavanagh are likewise from *Collected Pruse*, except where otherwise indicated.

3. John Coulson, *Newman and the Common Tradition* (Oxford University Press, 1964), p. 4.

4. Samuel Coleridge, quoted by A. E. Housman in his Leslie Stephen lecture of 1933 entitled 'The Name and Nature of Poetry'.

5. These are *Ascetic, Iniskeen Road: July Evening, Epic, Innocence, Kerr's Ass, The Hospital, The Self-Slaved, Question to Life* – all of them with their own spiritual innuendo.

6. Kavanagh describes technique as 'a method of getting at life'. Kavanagh wrote on the primacy of the 'ordinary': 'If I happen to meet a poet and I have met poets – I would expect him to reveal his powers of insight and imagination, even if he talked of poetry, farming, ground rents or any other commonplace subject. Above all I would expect to be excited and have my horizons of faith and hope widened by his ideas on the only subject that is of any real importance Man-in-the-world-and-why.'

7. Seamus Heaney, 'From Monaghan to the Grand Canal' in *Preoccupations*.

8. cf Northrop Frye, *The Double Vision, Language and Meaning in Religion* (University of Toronto Press, 1991).

9. It may be noted that Kavanagh wrote his prose and poetry before the issue of 'inclusive language' arose.

10. The Paschal Mystery: The Second Vatican Council, in its *Constitution on the Sacred Liturgy* (par 5) says of Christ: 'He achieved his task principally by the paschal mystery of the blessed passion, resurrection from the dead and glorious ascension, where by dying he destroyed our death and rising, he restored our life.' On a wider plane, the paschal mystery refers to the whole of salvation offered to human kind as an event which converts the whole history of men and women. Two stages may be distinguished in this event. The first refers to the paschal event as something which happened in time over two thousand years ago. The second refers to the way the paschal mystery exists in sacramental symbols today, that is, through its enactment in the liturgy. The word 'paschal' comes from the Greek *pascha* which, in turn, is derived from the Hebrew *pesach*, referring to the annual commemoration of Israel's first Passover in Egypt. This was the charter event that marked the Jewish people's liberation from bondage. The Jewish pasch is the memorialising of God's covenant with his people. In Christianity one is initiated into the paschal mystery through baptism. The death-resurrection motif is central to the life and liturgy of the Christian community. The pilgrimage of faith for all

is patterned on Jesus' passing over to God the Father, through his redemptive death and resurrection in which the followers of the Lord are incorporated.

11. The so called 'spiritualising tendency' is exemplified in what has become known as the Gnostic mindset. Gnosticism was an early heresy in Christianity and its particular intellectual and spiritual bias has continued to haunt mankind's quest for the Absolute. The teaching of Gnosticism involved a teaching of dualism between spirit and matter. The former was good, the latter evil. This attitude was a form of Syncretism, drawing from a mixture of Jewish, oriental sources, and an exaggerated version of earliest Christian elements, especially from one group within the primitive Christian community at Corinth. Gnosticism advocated an escape from a world of matter to the world of spirit. It tended towards what we would now call a snobby intellectualism, the original Greek word *gnosis* from which it was named, meaning knowledge. It claimed 'enlightenment' and something of a secret knowledge or a revelation concerning God and the source of all reality. It repudiated the possibility of the divine being rooted in or linked to the material in any form. It was both escapist and elitist in that it propounded a privileged, fast-track access to the deity. Gnosticism came to prominence in the second century AD, led by figures such as Marcian, Valentius, and Basilides. This hierarchy was vigorously opposed by second and third century church fathers, like Justin Martyr, Clement of Alexandria and notably by St Ireneus, the outstanding incarnationalist theologian. Near our own day the Gnostic bias surfaced in vestigial form in aspects of puritanism and even infiltrated strands of post-Tridentine Catholicism. A famous collection of Gnostic texts was rediscovered in 1945 near Nag-Hammadi, a Coptic site in Egypt.

12. The theologian Karl Rahner sj emphasises that the same reality is to be found in the mysteries of both the Trinity and the incarnation. The gift of what he calls 'God's self-communication' to us is central to his theology. The God who comes to us as Spirit, the Word of God and inexhaustible source, is God's own self. This restores the notion of manifestation to the theology of Trinity, or in other words restores the link between Trinity and incarnation.

13. Patrick Kavanagh's religious background. The three main sources of Patrick Kavanagh's religious formation were his home, his school and his parish. At home both his parents were strong in their attachment to their Catholic faith and passed on this inheritance as best they could to their son. The family, as a unit, was religious in the natural way of their day. One of Patrick's sisters, Cecilia, became a religious in the Presentation order, Sr Regius. In Kavanagh's parish there was the influential and colourful figure of the parish priest, Fr Bernard Maguire, who was pastor at Inniskeen from 1915 to 1948. The poet held Fr Maguire in both esteem and affection and wrote of him in *The Standard* newspaper in 1945 in a warm and appreciative way. He noted that Fr Maguire 'could talk about little bits of the gospel as if they could really happen'. He was a scholarly man who had formerly been rector of the Irish College at Salamanca in Spain. A good linguist, he is credited with translating John Henry Newman's *Idea of a University* into Spanish. For obvious reasons he was

nicknamed 'Salamanca Barney'. With very little real formal education (he left school in 3rd class), Kavanagh had acquired a lively sense of the gospel narrative, both at school at Kidnaminsha and from Fr Maguire's preaching. It is interesting that St Luke, with his infancy narratives, was his favourite evangelist. Kavanagh writes with some sagacity: 'A good idea of the nature of a poet is to be found in E. V. Rieu's introduction to his translations of the four gospels. He remarks of St Luke: "St Luke was a poet. I do not mean by this that he embroidered his narratives but rather that he knew how to distil truth from fact." Rieu goes on to refer to Luke's poetic insight into reality and to his realisation of the part played by woman in the revelation of the divine idea. That is the poetic mind.' Kavanagh learned prayers and hymns at school and knew the classic hymn to the Holy Spirit, *Veni Creator* (in Dryden's translation) by heart. His stable religious instruction came from the O'Reilly Catechism, the short, pithy answers of which he knew well. In adulthood Kavanagh read G. K. Chesterton, François Mauriac and other 'Catholic' writers of his day. He was acquainted with the writing of St Augustine, especially his *City of God*. He quoted approvingly from Augustine in a lecture to students at UCD: 'I am conscious of something within me that plays before my soul and is a light dancing in front of me. Were this brought to steadiness and perfection within me it would surely be eternal light.' Kavanagh probably read excerpts from St Thomas Aquinas and he was certainly familiar with the *Imitation of Christ* by Thomas à Kempis. It is reasonable to assume that he also dipped into other spiritual writers in his own way of reading which was patchy and spasmodic. On a wider level, it is worthwhile sketching the religious and theological climate that prevailed in the worldwide Catholic Church in Kavanagh's day. From 1907, the date of St Pius X's encyclical letter *Pascendi Dominici Gregis*, what one might call the way of sensibility in religious thinking, favoured by Augustine and indeed by Kavanagh himself, was to become suspect in the Catholic Church. Indeed this Pian regime prevailed, with some moderations, until the Second Vatican Council in 1962. This tight grip on Catholic thinking came about as a defensive reaction to the Catholic movement known as Modernism, which leaned towards an intuitive approach to Christian mystery, sometimes called the 'way of immanence'. The official Roman attitude was a strictly propositional view of revelation and a deductive relentlessly 'objective' method. There was little scope for theological impressionism. It treated the content of revelation as divine truth crystallised in theses formulated from scripture and the documents of tradition. It repudiated any experiential, affective or institutional mode of thought. That nurtured a kind of disembodied theology in the first half of the twentieth century. This religious climate, coming through in his parish church and elsewhere, would have given Kavanagh little encouragement in developing his personal style of religious understanding.

14. The God which Kavanagh discovered was 'the gay, imaginative God who made the fields and the trees and the flowers, a God not terribly to be feared.' (*Collected Pruse*) Moreover, in *Having Confessed* he reminds us that 'God must be allowed to surprise

us.' Further, he concludes that a purely speculative approach to God fails, if stripped of the 'flesh' of prayer:

> I am so glad
> To come so accidentally upon
> My Self at the end of a tortuous road
> And have learned with surprise that God
> Unworshipped withers to the Futile One. (*Auditors In*)

15. Kavanagh also declared: 'one must be ware of being too logical about anything. If we go on in a logical way we come to cage bars. We must not ask the question, "WHY is God?"' In *Advent* we find the lines:

> … we shall not ask for reasons payment
> The why of heart-breaking strangeness in dreeping hedges
> Nor analyse God's breath in common statement.

16. Kavanagh seems to be conscious of the value of interiority in the Christian life. He wrote: 'Basically we realise that all action is vulgar, that only the contemplative matters.' (*Collected Pruse*)

17. The way of unknowing in the mystical journey towards knowledge of God originates in developed form with the fifth-century Syrian monk whose *nom de plume* was Dionysius, in imitation of St Paul's acquaintance Dionysius the Areopagite. The Syrian writer has come to be referred to as the Pseudo-Dionysius. A scholar of neoplatonic thought, he influenced the Christian spiritual tradition through his treatise *Mystica Theologia*. This work spoke of concepts and symbols that led into a darkness which is the experience of God's love, and in which condition the soul is grasped by that love and transfigured. This may anticipate St John of the Cross' term 'The Dark Night of the Soul' eleven centuries later. Given the important role of the Pseudo-Dionysius in the formation of the Christian mystical tradition, it is significant to note that his writings in the Greek language were brought to the West by a ninth-century Irishman, John Scotus Eriugena, who translated them into Latin. Scotus, a layman, was one of the few who knew Greek at the time and he stands as a unique scholarly bridge between East and West. He was also a profound and original theological figure in his own right, especially renowned for his massive work *De Divisioni Naturae*, which deals with the entire panorama of life, created and uncreated reality. It works its way in metaphysical terms from inanimate nature right up to the Godhead.

18. Dom Cuthbert Butler OSB, a leading authority on mysticism, has written: 'There is probably no more misused word than "Mysticism".' Louis Dupré, another expert on the subject, suggests: 'No definition could be both meaningful and sufficiently comprehensive to include all experiences that at some point or other have been describes as "Mystical".' The Anglican mystical scholar N. R. Inge believed that no less that twenty-six separate definitions of mysticism could be formulated. One of the world's outstanding students of mysticism today is a Belfast-born Jesuit priest, Fr William Johnston, who for many years has been director of the Institute of

Oriental Religions at Sophia University in Tokyo. He is author of some ten books on the subject. In his monumental volume, *Mystical Theological – The Science of Love*, he attempts to update the mystical tradition of our day. He stresses the need for mysticism to go beyond a narrow concern for making people holy as individuals or as groups and become a catalyst for social and political change. Concerning reform in the Catholic Church, Johnston believes that beyond structural and juridical renewal, the church needs intellectual, moral and religious conversion and greater collaboration with the other world religions. Another Jesuit theologian, Karl Rahner, sees the experience of mystery as the indispensable core of the theological task. Since all are fundamentally God-targeted and God-touched, so all are a mystical people. Rahner has written: 'The Christian of the future will be a mystic or he or she will not exist at all, if by mysticism we mean a genuine experience of God, emerging at the very heart of our existence.' The innovative thinker Bernard Lonergan sj contends that even the very development of human consciousness is ultimately the result of God's love, driving the human being towards awareness and responsible living in an ever transformational relationship. On the other hand, the biblical scholar John McKenzie sounds a cautionary note concerning mystical manifestations: 'When mystics claim to have received information from Jesus himself about details from his life, especially detailed accounts of his passion, criticism deserves a very reserved attitude … in spite of the frequency of mystical experiences the official Roman Catholic Church is not sympathetic to mysticism and never has been. Mysticism like other things in the Roman Catholic Church changes with time and culture. It is extremely rare in the modern world … if the word credulous could be used in a neutral sense one can say that mysticism presupposes credulity.' Provocatively, McKenzie makes the strict point: '[Mysticism] is not the awareness of the divine which comes through faith, for faith is not a direct experience. But it is not the same as awareness of external reality which we have through the senses, for the object of the experience is not sensible.' He concludes: '[There is] no way to test the validity of mystical claims except the biblical maxim that the mystic is to be known by his or her fruits.' Despite McKenzie's reductionist views, it is clear that the mystical gift is multiform. With regard to Patrick Kavanagh, there can be no question but that he was endowed with a strong and authentic 'mystical imagination' as it has been called. For this reason the impressively researched and original treatment of Kavanagh in this context by Una Agnew ssl (*The Mystical Imagination of Patrick Kavanagh*, Dublin: Columba Press, 1998) is a most valuable contribution to Kavanagh studies.

19. Paradoxical language is a feature of the writings of the mystics. But paradox can be the idiom of profound truths even as it is evidenced in the teaching of Jesus Christ himself. Indeed the principle of contradiction in ordinary discourse is transcended in the realm of mystical utterance. The medieval mathematician and philosopher Nicholas of Cusa (d. 1464) is an important mentor in this matter, as he explains his understanding of what he calls 'the coincidence of opposites' in his book *The*

Vision of God. He also posits what he calls 'learnt ignorance' which is a condition of simplicity going beyond ratiocination to a level of intuition and understanding which enables one to embrace what is, on the face of it, incomprehensible, and a way of speaking what is ineffable. Nicholas of Cusa's teaching connects with Kavanagh's views on simplicity. It also illuminates the poet's penchant for particularity, as Cusa speaks of the 'contraction of the universe to the particular'. This he sees as 'the unfolding of the infinite in the finite and the enfolding of the finite in the infinite'. Again the mystical state of the 'nothingness' of St John of the Cross is somehow echoed in Kavanagh, who wrote: 'The apparent emptiness of experience may be its fullness. With experience we can take emptiness as a spiritual reality. We must take what is there even when it is nothing. As soon as one has excepted one's fate it becomes a richness.' (*Collected Prose*) A famous mystic, the Alexandrian Jew Philo, a contemporary of Jesus Christ, wrote: 'Sometimes when I have come to my work empty I have suddenly become full, ideas being in an invisible manner showered upon me and implanted in me from on high.' This statement moves in somewhat the same direction as Kavanagh's, though in a different language spoken 1500 years earlier and coming from a different continent.

20. Christianity and Hinduism: In India the issue of the 'the one and the many' has been expressed over the centuries in debates between the *advaita* (non-dualist) and *dvaita* (dualist) traditions. Advaitins hold that there is, in the last analysis, only one reality – Brahman the divine power. Dvaitins, on the other hand, hold that each soul has a separate existence on its own. Today advaita is associated mainly with the Vedanta school which is Hinduism's dominant religious philosophy which also influences much New Age thinking. Vedanta teaches that through spiritual discipline one may be brought to the non-dual mystical state of advaita, also called self-realisation. This is understood to be an experience of oneness that admits of no differentiation between oneself and all other beings, including God. In the dialogue between Christianity and the Hindu Vedanta over the past fifty years, the outstanding Christian figure has been the English Benedictine Bede Griffiths and his more radical confrère, the French priest Henri Le Saux, who received initiation as a Hindu *sannyasin* or renunciate, and soon after claimed to have experienced advaita, the complete and radical oneness with God in which all duality is dissolved. Le Saux went on to assert that this, too, was the experience that Jesus had in a pre-eminent manner as he uttered the words 'I and the Father are one'. The uniqueness of Jesus, as held by Christians, is corroborated, as it happens, by the Dalai Lama, who holds that Jesus, unlike Hindu or Buddhist mystics, did not need to evolve spiritually through a number of stages from ordinary human awareness to one of enlightenment and oneness with God. It seems that in the state of advaita, when all forms of duality are superseded, there is no Other to whom one can pray. Yet outstanding Hindus, such as Gandhi and Tagore, prayed to God to the end of their lives. Incidentally, Kavanagh, who had been introduced to the Upanishads, the Hindu scriptures, by A. E. Russell, remarked: 'It was a pity that he should have

buried his authentic genius in the vasty deeps of the Upanishads.' (Quoted by Alan Warner in his book, *Apocalypse of Clay.*) In the Buddhist tradition there is no real difference to be found between the world of sense and the state of enlightenment which is called Nirvana, that is, the ultimate emptiness.

21. Sufism: The Sufi component of the Muslim faith is gently poetic and contemplative. For ideological reasons it has been spurned by the *ulamas* or teachers of the sterner and more legalistic Islamic religious currents. A notable convergence is to be found in the Sufi and Christian medieval mystical literature, for instance, between the outstanding Persian mystic, Al Ghazzali (d. 1111) and St Bernard of Clairveaux (d. 1153), and between the legendary thirteenth-century woman Sufi, Radi'a of Basra, who has been called the Muslim St Teresa of Avila (d. 1380), and Christian contemplatives in Europe. A wealth of Islamic mystical writing has been preserved and widely published in recent years. The scholastics were, of course, indebted in this and other respects to the Arab scholars who first introduced Greek writings to medieval Christendom. Foremost in this critical intellectual transmission were the renowned Avicenna or Ibn Sina (d. 1037) and Averroes or Ibn Rushd (d. 1188). In particular, it is well to remember the substantial Islamic mystical prayer heritage enjoyed by Europe, which originated in Iraq, Iran, Turkey and other Middle Eastern locations. This mainly Arabic quest, like Kavanagh's, was primarily that of union with the God of Abraham, as was the poet's with the self-same God of Jesus Christ. Yet another connection with Christian mysticism comes from the Alexandrian Jewish luminary Philo and his school, as well as elements from the Kabala tradition. European Catholic scholars have long been conversant with the treasures of Sufi thought. I remember, as a student, attending a Christian-Muslim conference at Azrou, near Meknes, Morocco in 1957, where I met the then elderly French Arabic scholar Louis Massignon, who among other things had been a close friend of Charles de Foucauld, the famous French hermit who had lived in North Africa. Massignon told me that such was his (Massignon's) regard for the Sufi tradition that he had wanted, above all, to celebrate the Christian mysteries in the Arab language of the Sufi holy men. For that reason Massignon, a married man, had received special permission to be ordained a priest in the Melchite (Arab language) Rite – a dramatic example perhaps of inter-faith fervour on the part of the Reverend M. Massignon. I remember serving his Mass in that rite at the Benedictine monastery of Toumliline at Azrou, which hosted the conference in question.

    I also recall Patrick Kavanagh telling me in conversation how much the Muslim tradition appealed to him. I suspect he was referring to the Sufi strand in particular.

22. This theme is explained by Mircea Eliade in his book *The Scared and the Profane – The Nature of Religions* (New York: Harper and Row, 1959).

23. Concerning Kavanagh's claim that comedy is abundance of life, he added: 'to write lively verse or prose to be involved with comedy requires enormous physical and mental power. Energy as Blake remarked is "eternal delight". The more energy is in a poem or prose work the more comic it is.' (*Collected Pruse*)

24. Dante's *Divine Comedy*: In *Imaginative literature 1* (Great Books Series) *From Homer to Shakespeare*, Mortimer Adler and Seymour Cain wrote of Dante's *Divine Comedy*: 'It is called a comedy because it has a happy ending – redemption … Dante uses historical persons as characters in his fictional story to express spiritual and moral truths that transcend history and fiction. For this 'comedy' is deadly serious … Dante said that the real subject of the work is man's freedom of choice and his responsibility for his moral attainments and failings … The *Divine Comedy* is a human comedy and its subject is man as a moral being.'

25. The Comic Vision: cf *The Comedy of Revelation* by Francesca A. Murphy (T. and T. Clark, Edinburgh, 2000). In the section entitled 'The Human and Divine Comedy', Murphy paraphrases the critic Northrop Frye: 'Northrop Frye argued that the comic plot always follows an upward moving U. In its downward graph – the first stroke of the U – the plot moves away from a good situation and towards conflict and suffering. In its upward graph, the second stroke, the plot turns towards happiness and communal festivity. In a dramatic action, each unfolding event drives the next and is contained in it. In tragic drama, a coalition of fate and hubris are mobilising the events. In comic drama, each scene is propelled forward by desire and by grace. At the summit of Frye's U stands the recovery of community: the good city is what we desire most.'

26. Kavanagh reminded us that 'Shakespeare lived on the capital of Christianity, Cervantes within it.' (*Collected Pruse*)

27. cf *The Feast of Fools*, Section 5: 'Christ as Harlequin', by Harvey Cox (Harvard University Press, 1969). Also John Huizingas *Homo Ludens, Man at Play* by Hugo Rahner sj (New York: Herder and Herder, 1967), *The Bias of Comedy and the Narrow Escape into Faith* by Nathan A. Scott (*The Christian Scholar*, no. 44, Spring 1961). Apposite here is the quote: 'For the foolishness of God is wiser than men and the weakness of God is stronger than men.' (1 Cor 1:25)

28. Kavanagh wrote: 'Not caring is really a sense of values and feeling of confidence … a man who cares is not the master.' (*Collected Pruse*)

29. Kavanagh further contextualises the gift of simplicity as it first began and eventually returned in its mature and final form. He wrote: 'Thirty years earlier Shancoduff's watery hills could have done the trick, but I was too thick to take the hint. Curious, how I had started off with the right simplicity indifferent to crude reason and then ploughed my way through complexities and anger, hatred and ill will towards the faults of men and came back to where I started. For one of the very earliest things I wrote, even predating Shancoduff, started this way:

> Child do not go
> Into the dark places of soul,
> For there the grey wolves whine,
> The lean grey wolves. (*To a Child*)

In that little thing I had become airborne and more, I had achieved weightlessness.' (*Collected Pruse*)

30. Kavanagh declared: 'But one must not allow oneself to be inhibited by too precise a definition.' (*Collected Pruse*)

31. A relationship with God in Jesus Christ, however this may be defined, is necessary for salvation. 'I am the vine, you are the branches. Whoever remains in me, with me in him, bears fruit in plenty; for cut off from me you can do nothing.' (John 15:5) Pelagius (d. p. 418), a lay monk who taught that one could be saved by virtue of one's own human capacity. This runs counter to the universal understanding of the Christian church that God's grace, which is an unmerited gift, must always be operative in the journey towards salvation.

Alphabetical Index of Titles

238

Index of First Lines